Christie's
JOURNEY
The Beat Goes On

D1004497

JOHN R. BAIN

ISBN 978-1-0980-7829-4 (paperback)
ISBN 978-1-0980-7830-0 (digital)

Christian Faith Publishing, Inc.
832 Park Avenue
Meadville, PA 16335
www.christianfaithpublishing.com

Author photo by Joni DeMoss

Printed in the United States of America

To our Lord and Savior, Jesus Christ, as well as Christie, Brian, Natalie, Westin, Sean, and my best friend forever and love of my life Andrea. And to my father, Russell. Dad, I thank you for teaching me patience, love, discipline, and forgiveness when I was growing up even though I didn't always know it at the time.

ACKNOWLEDGMENTS

Thank you to my daughter, Christie; you are so strong, brave, and beautiful. Thank you for reliving moments that were uncomfortable for you so I could share your story. To Andrea, my wife; Sweet Cheeks, you are my rock, and the rock of our family. I love you. Thank you to my son, Sean, for being the good man that you are. You make your mother and I proud of you every day. To my Aunt Lora; thank you for being a fact-checker in this writing process and your moments of collaboration. They were truly inspirational. To Patty Hepner, thank you for reading this work when it was in progress and for your wonderful words of encouragement, I truly appreciate it. To everyone that helped us during the difficult time we went through, by your good thoughts and prayers. To our angel here on Earth, Paula Simmons, we are forever grateful to you for caring for Natalie and Westin. Dean Renae McCray, thank you for giving Christie a chance. To Officer Michael Wade, you are truly a hero to our family. To Dr. Kevin Hayes, Dr. Gregory White, Dr. Hani Najm, and all of the medical personnel at Christus St. Michael and the Cleveland Clinic, thank you. And to our Lord, father in heaven, I thank you for your Grace.

1

June 9, 2019

John and Andrea Bain had a great week with their granddaughter, Natalie Firth, a seven-year-old going on fourteen, at their home just north of Wayland, Iowa. Natalie has been in their lives now since she was just a couple of months shy of two years old, and it was instant unconditional love and acceptance from all, and John became Papa John and Andrea is now Gigi to this smart and beautiful little lady.

The three were on their way to Poplar Bluff, Missouri, to meet up with Natalie's dad, mom, and little brother. Natalie's dad is Brian Firth, age thirty-two; her mom is Christie Firth, age twenty-nine; and little Westin John Firth, not quite three months old, is her little brother.

The reason for the meeting in Poplar Bluff is that it is a little over halfway from Wayland, Iowa, to Simms, Texas, where the Firths live. Total drive time one way from one place to the other is about twelve hours with gasoline stops and a meal stop. It's always a bittersweet time to get together because there is never enough time to spend with each other. Work duties and the like make for shorter visits, and many families know that feeling and experience. But all three heading back from the north to the south were just as excited as the three coming from the south to the north.

They all arrived on time at the arranged meeting place, the Holiday Inn Express, and then headed to lunch. It was going to be a wonderful visit but way too short. All four adults had to be back to work the next day bright and early.

They had a great visit. John told his daughter Christie how beautiful she looked and how amazing things are going for her after just having the baby. Christie was so proud of Westin and how well he was doing too. Brian was a proud father, and you could tell he was very happy also. Andrea was holding little Westin and feeding him a bottle while Natalie told of her past week's adventures of going to the zoo, shopping, swimming, fishing, and wrapping up her week the night before at a classic car cruise-in in Washington, Iowa, where she helped Gigi and Papa John sell 50/50 raffle tickets for the car club, all the while with a cast on her left arm from falling down on the playground a few weeks back.

John and Andrea both noticed some pinkish/red splotches on Christie's skin, around her collarbone and on a few different places on both her arms. They asked her what she thought it was but she didn't know. She promised she would get them checked.

It was time to go. Hugs were exchanged from all present. Papa John did everything he could to hold back his tears but to no avail. Every time they say goodbye he cries. He has always had a hard time saying goodbye to Christie, and now she has added three more people into his life to make it even harder. Gigi does a better job holding back the tears but is just as torn up as Papa John.

On the way home, John and Andrea talked about the happy little family from Texas, and how proud they are of them. As the miles continued, they started talking about the upcoming work week. Andrea had been on vacation from her job at the Rock Island Arsenal and would have to be back on the road on Monday morning by four in order to get to work on time by 6:00 a.m. John would be at his job at KCII Radio in Washington, Iowa, at 7:30 a.m.

On the way back to Texas, the kids fell asleep rather quickly. Christie discussed with Brian how hard it was going back to work after being with Westin on maternity leave. Like most mothers they worry that their child is in the proper care, won't miss them too much, or, even worse, forget them. Christie realized though that her contribution of employment at the Red River Credit Union Call

Center ensured bills were paid and her family had health insurance, and as we all know that is very important to all families.

Brian assured her that all will be okay. Brian is in business with his father, John "Butch" Firth. They run a logging business. In the Texarkana, New Boston, and Simms area in Northeast Texas, there are many mills that need to be supplied and many areas where trees need to be downed. It's hard work that at times is very lucrative and other times very expensive. Equipment in the logging business is not cheap and breakdowns happen too frequently.

All parties made it home that evening and called each other to let them know they had arrived. Monday morning would come fast but the trip was worth it.

2

Christie Bain was working at Honeywell, a private contractor with the US Army, at the Rock Island Arsenal in Rock Island, Illinois, in the early months of 2012. She was making a very good salary for someone fresh out of college. Christie recently graduated from St. Ambrose University in Davenport, Iowa. It is a smaller private college where she excelled in her studies. She earned her bachelor of arts degree with a double major in Business Management and Marketing.

A few months into her job with Honeywell, Christie got the impression that she, along with a few others, might be getting laid off. With student loans and a recently purchased Dodge Nitro to pay for along with rent and everything else, Christie was fretful. Then one day at work she saw an opening within Honeywell to work in Kuwait. The job would pay $100,000 per year. She applied for the position and then went to visit her parents to tell them the potential news. At this time John and Andrea Bain were living in Bettendorf, Iowa, where they had their family home built back in 1994. Christie didn't live far away in the same town, and her older brother, Sean, was currently living back home with mom and dad after graduating college in 2010 from St. Ambrose University. He as well had a Business Management bachelor of arts degree. Sean also worked at the Rock Island Arsenal where he interned there while in college and now currently works for the US Army as a civilian.

Christie arrived at her parents' house to tell them the news. Christie walked in and gave her mom and dad a hug and then told them the "news."

"You know how I told you two that I might become unemployed soon?"

John and Andrea replied, "Yes."

"Well, I have put a stop to that!"

John asked, "How so, did you get a new job?"

"I applied for a different position with Honeywell. I will be making sure the troops that come from the US or leaving the Middle East have all of their personnel actions in order."

Andrea said, "That sounds like a very good position. Good for you!"

John asked, "What's the catch?"

Christie responds sheepishly and says, "I will have to live in Kuwait."

John responded like many overprotective fathers would, "Ah, I don't think so young lady! I am not having my daughter over in a war zone! Not on my watch!"

Christie responded, "Dad, I'm an adult! I'm no longer on your watch! I take care of myself! This is an opportunity for me to make a lot of money, so much so that I can pay off my new car and my student loans all within a year. Plus, I'll be helping our soldiers. I'll be on the biggest US Military base over there, Camp Arifjan."

John replied, "Well I don't like it."

Christie said, "It may not happen but if it does you will have to learn to accept it."

It happened. Christie was hired. She would be a management analyst for the 402nd AFSB SWA in Kuwait. She would be leaving for Kuwait, with a quick stop in Germany first, soon after training in Indiana. Her training at Camp Atterbury in Edinburgh, Indiana, was a mini boot camp of sorts where she trained in using gas masks, what to look for as unusual in a country that would be completely unusual to her, as well as freeing herself from an overturned Jeep. On the way there, she thought she was on the wrong bus since she was the only woman on it. Once there, she shared barracks quarters with fifty other women. Her duffle bag had a bulletproof vest, a helmet, and some other survival equipment. It was as big as her both in height and weight. She left in late March of 2012. John and Andrea saw their "baby girl" off on her adventure at the Quad City International Airport in Moline, Illinois. They both teared up at this goodbye.

Nearly six years prior its inception, the 402nd AFSB, started at Logistic Support Element-Iraq.[1] At least she wouldn't be in Iraq.

Christie flew in a C-10 airplane to Kuwait from Germany. The plane landed in the night. Christie and the other passengers were loaded up onto big busses. She couldn't see out the windows, and no one could see in them, it frightened Christie. They proceeded to an air force base and she was told that someone would come and get her. A Kuwaiti gentleman working for the US government took her in a car to her apartment in Kuwait City.

Brian Firth worked for TACOM (The United States Army Tank-automotive and Armaments Command) working on the CROWS (Common Remotely Operated Weapons Station) mission. He was a civilian working on the travel team for the Red River Army Depot out of Hooks, Texas. Brian installed CROWS weapon systems on MRAPs (Mine-Resistant Ambush Protected) and MATVs (MRAP All-Terrain Vehicle) as a mechanic. He traveled back and forth from Iraq and Kuwait to Texas. He spent four and a half years in Iraq and one year in Kuwait and also was in and out of Afghanistan several times. The job was very lucrative for a young man from Texas with a humble upbringing. Brian did well with the money he earned during this time. He even built a ranch-style home on some property he purchased out in the country in Simms, Texas.

One morning shortly after Christie arrived in Kuwait and working in her office in the *million-dollar tent*, she got a visit from two men named Brian. Brian Firth referred to his buddy Bryan Idalski as B2. Today was B2's day to start out processing. B2 was looking forward to going back home to Michigan, and Brian Firth was looking forward to getting to know the pretty blond-haired girl much better as he joked around with her and made B2 the "butt" of his jokes. Brian Firth was also starting the out-processing procedure to go to Afghanistan. Out-processing usually is a one-visit event. For

---

[1] Information courtesy of the US Army-article by Capt. Avery W. Evans, HHD commander, 402nd AFSB.

the Brians it was extended to three days. The gents didn't always have their paperwork completely together and had to keep coming back. That was a good way for Brian to continue to visit with Christie. In order for the men to even get to Christie's office, they had to go through two security checkpoints. Once the processing process was over, Brian asked for her phone number, and Christie couldn't remember her actual cell phone number and gave her Magic Jack Internet phone number. Brian wrote down his phone number and told Christie if she would like to hang out sometime to give him a call. Christie thought this tall good-looking man with tattoos up and down his arms "sleeves" and some showing on his neck had the look of a soldier and she was interested in finding out more about him. Instead of going to Afghanistan, Brian decided to stay in Kuwait.

Several weeks later in May, John was at work and got a call from Brian. They had minor conversations in the past via Skype when Christie would call, so it wasn't a complete surprise. "Hello, sir, this is Brian Firth."

"Hi, Brian, is everything okay?"

"Yes, sir. Everything is really good. I was calling today to get your blessing to marry Christie."

John was somewhat surprised. He replied, "How can I give my blessing to someone I have never met in person? I'm sure you're a good guy or my daughter wouldn't be interested in you, but I can't give my blessing this way. You have a daughter. What's her name?"

Brian replied, "Natalie, sir."

John responded, "Let's go forward a few years. If Natalie is dating someone, and they are getting close and want to get married, if her boyfriend called you on the telephone from halfway around the world, and you never got to meet him in person, or even shook his hand, would you give your blessing?"

Brian replied, "No, sir, I wouldn't. I understand."

John said, "Now all that being said, you two could get upset with me and do what you want. You're both adults. Just know, if you are engaged without my blessing, that is going to be hard to have a decent relationship with you."

Brian responded, "Sir, you have my word. We will not be engaged without your blessing."

John smiled and said, "Brian, thank you for that. Also, thank you for calling me. A lot of young men in today's world would not do that. I truly appreciate it. I hope I get to meet you sooner than later. You be safe over there and please look out for my girl."

"Oh, I will, sir. Thank you."

John hung up his phone and breathed a sigh.

Christmastime 2012 came, and John and Andrea had the best present ever. Christie was coming home for a visit! They picked her up at the O'Hare Airport in Chicago, Illinois.

Christie had a big smile on her face when they all were in the car on their way home to Bettendorf. She said, "I have some news." John looked into the rearview mirror and said, "Come on, don't leave us hanging, what is it?"

With a big beautiful smile on her face Christie said, "I may not have to go back to Kuwait after Christmas."

Andrea smiled and John said, "That's the best news ever! How is this coming about?"

Christie replied, "Well, I may be getting laid off. So, I've got all my stuff already packed in boxes and addressed and ready to go so if I get the news while I'm here, I will contact my roommate in Kuwait, and she will send them this way."

John in his best Santa Claus impersonation yelled, "Merry Christmas!"

Brian arrived in Bettendorf the day after Christmas. He was on a mission. He wanted John's blessing so he could ask Christie to marry him. After spending a full day with John and Andrea, they realized this was a good young man. John gave Brian his blessing on December 27, and Christie had a big beautiful engagement ring on her finger quickly after that. Brian was so relieved when John gave him his blessing he responded, "Thank you, sir. I didn't think you would like me with all of my tattoos."

John grinned and said, "I don't judge people by their tattoos and nipple rings. I determine what a person is like by getting to know them, and I'm going to be proud to have you as my son-in-law." The two men shook hands.

Brian was done with his contract in Kuwait and stayed home in Texas. Christie had to return to Kuwait. When she arrived, her roommate asked what she was doing back since she had been laid off. Christie had not received the information and made a trip half-way round the world to receive this news. She quickly made arrangements to get back to the United States and more specifically to start a new chapter in her life with Brian in Texas.

They were married on a very hot day in a beautiful outdoor setting in Arkansas on June 21, 2014. John gave away his daughter. He made sure she knew that this was not a goodbye. It was a happy day.

3

June 11, 2019

It was a beautiful day in Texas. Christie dropped off Westin at the babysitter's house and headed into work at the Red River Credit Union located on the Red River Army Depot in Hooks, Texas. Christie texted her brother Sean. She asked, "Have you got dad a Father's Day gift yet?"

Sean replied, "There is a new app from DC Comics that is kind of cool. It will give him access to all the DC Comics ever made in digital form as well as the new shows and a lot of the old ones."

Christie said, "Count me in." Christie thought, *Thanks Sean, now I don't have to worry about getting something for dad and getting it up to Iowa by Father's Day.* Andrea's birthday was tomorrow and the two kids had gotten their mother a gift certificate for a "well-deserved" massage. With a new baby, a full-time job, and then handling the paperwork for the logging business; this young mother was plenty busy.

One of Christie's coworkers, Cynthea Vickery, stopped by Christie's office to check in. They are close friends and keep tabs with each other throughout the day as well as outside of work. Cynthea told Christie that she was feeling kind of tired, and Christie said she was too. Christie mentioned how much drive time she and Brian and the kids had on Sunday and that she was still wore out from that, as well as keeping up with feedings for Westin and his baby sleeping schedule. Christie was worn out.

It was a beautiful day in Iowa too. John was sitting at his desk at KCII Radio around 8:30 a.m. when he received a text from Sean telling him about the neat Father's Day gift, he was getting from Sean and Christie. Sean said that it was all setup and ready to go and that John should receive an e-mail, and Sean didn't want him thinking it was spam or something. John thanked him and thought to himself that he will have to call Christie later and thank her too.

The workday continued. It was getting close to closing time just around 4:30 p.m. Christie and Cynthea were both looking forward to five o'clock closing time for the day. Cynthea's office is right next to Christie's. Cynthea could hear Christie on the phone. It sounded like a personal call more than work related. Cynthea noticed that Christie had suddenly stopped talking. There was no "thanks, have a great day, talk to you later" or anything. *Bang!* Cynthea heard a loud noise followed by another bang not as loud followed by a crash. Cynthea yelled out, "Christie!" There was no response and Cynthea called out her name again. Still no response. Suddenly there was a noise that came from Christie's office that sounded like snoring but a lot worse. The noise stopped and Cynthea entered Christie's office. Christie was lying face down on the floor in a pool of her own blood.

In that moment Cynthea had no idea what to do. Cynthea ran to the office next to hers and told her coworker to head toward Christie's office while she went on to get the acting supervisor at the time because they are the one to unlock the building to allow emergency personnel to enter. Cynthea grabbed her phone and called 911. The coworkers all tried to get Christie's attention as well as trying to get her to respond. The 911 dispatcher instructed them to roll her on her back. Christie could not respond. The next thing they were instructed to do was to see if she was breathing. She was sort of gasping but not breathing. Her body was trying to breath in the oxygen it needed but couldn't. One of her coworkers grabbed Christie's jacket from her chair to use to apply pressure on her temple where she was bleeding from. There was also blood from her mouth. The 911 dispatcher told Cynthea that they needed to start CPR (cardio-pulmonary resuscitation) because she wasn't breathing, and her skin tone had started turning blue. It was bad. Christie was gone. Cynthea stayed on the phone while coworker Dean Renae McCray started CPR. She didn't have to do CPR for long. Another coworker went outside and flagged down a Red River Depot Police Officer who happened to be driving by.

Officer Michael Wade called in what was happening to his base so they could inform fire and rescue. He then ran into the Credit Union Call Center and quickly took over CPR duties. Soon after that the paramedics from the fire and rescue took over. Christie started breathing shortly after the paramedics took over. The paramedics loaded Christie into the ambulance for her trip to Christus St. Michael Hospital in Texarkana. Cynthea called Brian to let him know Christie was in trouble. Brian was working outside of Atlanta, Texas, and his cell phone service was not the best there. Cynthea didn't want to overwhelm him since he would be driving quite a way to get to the hospital in Texarkana. She told him that Christie had passed out at work and was being rushed to Christus St. Michael Hospital. It was 4:45 p.m. Everything happened so quickly.

The Credit Union Call Center employees were all in shock. It had been a mad house. Acting Supervisor Nola told everyone to finish out the day. She gathered Christie's belongings and headed to the hospital. Cynthea thanked God for being as "nosey" as she is, because there were others in the building that heard the noises too but didn't think anything of it.

Brian left the work site and headed toward the hospital. He decided he better call Iowa and let the family know what was going on. He dialed his mother-in-law Andrea to tell her the news. As the phone was dialing, he was trying to think of what to tell her. He didn't know what was actually wrong with Christie except that she had passed out at work and was being taken by ambulance to the hospital. Andrea didn't answer her phone. Brian tried several times to no avail.

John Bain had a very good day and was heading home from work on time for a change. Something that is much-appreciated. John was in his car and not far from home when he received a call from his son-in-law, Brian. John thought this was a little unusual because Brian doesn't call that often, Christie usually does the dialing. He hoped everything was okay or if it was a butt-dial that would be okay too. He received a pocket dial from Brian earlier in the day and they exchanged texts letting each other know all was okay and to both have a good day. John answered the phone, "Hi, Brian, what's happening?" Brian responded in a somber tone, "Hello, Mr. John, I've got some bad news." John urged Brian to tell him what was going on. "I got a call from Christie's work. She passed out and she is in an ambulance on her way to the hospital in Texarkana."

John didn't know what to think. He asked Brian, "Do they know what caused her to pass out?"

Brian said, "No sir, they don't."

John told Brian to drive carefully and to call back as soon as he knew something more. John immediately called Andrea. Andrea did not answer her cell phone. She was at work in Rock Island and it was hard to say where she would be exactly in this hour.

John arrived home about 5:20 p.m. and got a hold of Andrea on the phone. He told her what he knew. Andrea said to John, "We've got to get down there. Can you check on flights from Cedar Rapids?" John said he would. He told Andrea to just worry about getting home as quickly as possible and to drive carefully. He told her he loved her.

John checked with a couple of different airlines to get to either Texarkana or Dallas. The quickest would have them arriving in Dallas at 7:30 a.m. the next morning after having to fly to Chicago and then New Jersey. They would then have to acquire a rental car and then drive two hours northeast to Texarkana. John determined they would be driving to Texarkana and there would not be a lot of stops. He started packing a bag. John realized his car needed gas. He headed into Wayland to fill up. This will be one less thing to worry about as they head down the road to Texas.

Lora Bain, John's aunt, and Andrea and John's neighbor was preparing dinner for her and her brother, Donald. It was chicken Alfredo and it was looking and smelling delicious. Her phone rang. It was John. Usually Lora doesn't answer her phone when she is in the middle of things and usually calls back as soon as she gets to a stopping point. This time she answered, "Hello." There was no response from John on the other end. "John, are you there? Where are you?"

John just barely gets the words out. His voice is not normal. "I'm at the BP in Wayland. It's Christie, she has had an accident at work. She passed out and hit her head on the office safe. They are taking her to the hospital in Texas."

Lora could tell that John wasn't in a good state of mind at the moment. She asked, "Do you want me to come over?"

John replied, "No, thanks. Andrea is on her way home and as soon as she gets there she will pack and then we are heading out. Could you get our mail for us and keep an eye on the house while we're gone? Also, call your sisters in the Quad Cities as well as Uncle Gary and anybody else that should know." They come from a large extended family and having Lora make the calls would be a big help.

Lora responded, "Yes, I'll take care of all of that. You guys drive carefully and focus on Christie."

John thanked her and hung up. He was back at his house.

Lora's first call was to her pastor, Dave Schooley, of the Eicher Emmanuel Mennonite Church. She gave what details she had about Christie and asked him to include her in the church's prayer chain. Pastor Dave responded that he most certainly would. Lora then started calling her sisters.

Andrea called Brian while driving home to Wayland. "How are things going, Brian?"

Brian responded, "Ma'am, they are saying she had a cardiac arrest and they don't know..." Brian couldn't speak. He handed the phone to the doctor. The doctor introduced himself, "Ma'am, this is Dr. Kevin Hayes, I understand you are Christie's mother?" Andrea responded that she was. Dr. Hayes continued, "Christie has had a cardiac arrest and is currently in stable but critical condition here in the ICU of Christus St. Michael Hospital in Texarkana, Texas." Andrea thanked Dr. Hayes and told him that they would be on their way.

Andrea called John. She was still about forty-five minutes away from home. John told her that he couldn't find any flights and they would be heading to Texas as soon as she got home and packed. Andrea relayed to John what Dr. Hayes had told her. John replied, "Oh God! Andrea, we have to get down there. Please hurry home. Be careful on the roads." They were both crying. She said she would be home soon and she would be careful. John was in his dining room when he hung up with Andrea. He dropped to his knees and started praying, "Dear Heavenly Father, please look after Christie and keep her safe. Please let the doctors do the right things to help her. Lord, please don't take our Christie from us. Please, please, please Lord, please let her be okay. Her baby Westin needs her, Brian needs her, Natalie needs her and Andrea, Sean and I need her. Please Lord don't take her from us. In Jesus's name I pray, Amen."

As Andrea drove toward home, she was frantic. She called her good friend Rose Reasor and told her what had happened. Andrea told Rose that John was checking on flights to get them to Texarkana but wasn't having any luck. Rose told Andrea, "I've got a friend that is a travel agent. I'll call her and I'll look into it as well and let you know what is available." Andrea thanked her friend. She then realized that she needed to let her brother know as well. Andrea called her brother, Chris Carlson. Chris had just completed his work day and was relaxing at his home in Rock Island. Chris answered his phone, "Hey, Sis, what's up?" Andrea tried to compose her voice the best that she could. She said, "Christie is in trouble. She went into cardiac arrest at work. They transported her in an ambulance to a hospital in Texarkana. She is in stable but critical condition right now." Chris was stunned. Christie is his only niece. He responded, "Oh no, how can I help?" Andrea told him to pray for her. Andrea and Chris had recently lost their older sister, Beth Carlson, back on February 25, this year and her passing had been devastating to them and the rest of their family. Beth wasn't married and did not have any children, so settling her estate became the responsibility of Chris and Andrea's. Their parents, Bob and Jean, passed away in 2007, Bob on February 15 and Jean on April 2. Andrea and Chris are what is left from this nuclear family.

Beth was a very caring person who liked to lavish her family and friends with gifts. Beth loved to shop. Throughout their years growing up, Beth always doted on Christie and Sean and they always were given the latest clothing fashions and toys from their aunt Beth.

Chris told Andrea to please keep him informed and he hoped and prayed that Christie would get through this okay. Andrea thanked her younger brother and focused on the drive as best that she could.

Rose called Andrea. She and the travel agent were finding the same thing that John had. There was no quick way to fly to Texarkana from Iowa. Andrea thanked her friend and realized the drive would be the quickest way to get to Christie.

It was a little after 6:00 p.m. John texted Brian. "How are you two doing? Andrea and I will be on our way down as soon as she gets to my house."

Brian texted back, "All right I hadn't got to see her or anything yet."

John replied back, "Can you talk or would you rather text?"

Brian responded; "I can talk." John called Brian. There had been no updates since Brian had spoken to Andrea. John told Brian to pray for Christie and that they would be there soon. He also told Brian he loves him. John asked where Westin was, and Brian said he was at Rhonda's house and he was doing fine. John told Brian it was good that they have such nice friends and that Andrea and he would be on the way soon.

John was thinking about what needed to be done next. He double-checked doors to make sure they were locked. He turned on a light that would make it appear that someone was home during the nighttime hours. He paced the house. He needed to call Sean.

Sean Bain was excited! Singer Sir Paul McCartney was performing in Moline, Illinois, tonight and Sean was going to be there. Sean's phone rang. It was his dad calling. Sean didn't want to pick up the phone since he was getting ready for the big concert. He decided to answer anyway since his dad was excited for him going too. Sean picked up the phone, "Hi, Dad."

John answered, it was hard to speak, "Sean, your sister is in the hospital in Texarkana. She went into cardiac arrest at work. It's not good. Your mom and I are heading there as soon as she gets here."

Sean responded, "I just talked to her today. We got that Father's Day gift for you and a birthday gift for mom. She was fine. What should I do? Should I go with you and mom?"

John answered, "No. Stay and go to the concert. There isn't anything that can be done right now. Let us get down there, and then we can tell you if you should come down or not."

Sean said, "Okay. I hope Christie is okay. I love you, Dad."

John said, "I love you, Son." They hung up. John started pacing again. He needed to call Joe.

Joe Bain is John's younger brother. They have a middle sister, Joan DeMoss. Their father, Russell, passed away twenty-two years ago, a victim of cancer. Their mother, Beverly, now seventy-five years old was doing well and living in Davenport, Iowa. John was barely able to speak and he knew if he tried to call his mom or sister that it would be worse. He told Joe what was going on right now. Joe was choked up. After all, Christie was his first niece and he always had a special place in his heart for her and would do anything for her. Joe asked if he should head toward Texas and John told him not at this time. John asked Joe to call their mother and sister to let them know what is going on, and he asked them all to pray for Christie. Joe wished his brother the best and hung up so that he could contact Beverly and Joni.

Andrea arrived at their home. John hugged her and then she hurriedly packed and they were out the door. She plugged the address of Christus St. Michael Hospital into the GPS of the car and away they went not knowing if Christie would survive the night.

Paula Simmons, Christie's best friend, had received a voicemail from a coworker of Christie's, Joyce Lawrence, that Paula needed to call her as soon as possible. Paula returned Joyce's call and Joyce told Paula to sit down and then proceeded to tell Paula what had happened to Christie. Paula was in shock. She knew she had to get to her friend right away. Along with her husband, Daniel, she quickly headed to the hospital to check on their friend. On the way there, Paula posted the following on Facebook: "Prayer requests right now, don't ask questions." She didn't tag Christie or anyone else in the post.

4

John and Andrea didn't say much as they made their way to Texas. Every once in a while, he would look over at Andrea and she was wiping tears off her cheeks. It always tore him up to see his wife cry. Fortunately, it didn't happen often. He held her hand and kept focused on getting to Christie. John couldn't help himself, and he too would start crying. Andrea rubbed his shoulder and asked him if he wanted her to drive. John told her thanks but he needed to drive as he pulled himself together.

At Christus St. Michael Hospital in Texarkana, Texas, Dr. Kevin R. Hayes, MD, entered the following information onto an Electrophysiology Consultation Form:

General
Date and Time
Consult Documented on June 11, 2019 at 18:10 by the following provider: Kevin R. Hayes, MD
Attending Physician:
Patient Admission date:
Chief Complaint: VF arrest
Reviewed patient's chart: Yes
HPI
Source: Patient, Family, ED Physician, EMS, Old Medical Record
History of Present Illness
Ms. Firth/Finn is an unfortunate twenty-nine-year-old woman who is three months postpartum who is currently in the emergency department critically ill after having an out-of-hospital arrest.

24

Obviously she is unable to give any history. EMS reports that they were called to her place of business this afternoon when she was sitting in her chair and suddenly slumped backward. A police officer was a first responder and began performing chest compressions immediately. By time EMS got there and AED was applied and showed frank ventricular fibrillation. One external defibrillation converted her to what appears to be atrial fibrillation by the rhythm strips. CPR was continued in route because she had no palpable pulse. By time she got to the emergency department she had restoration of spontaneous circulation after receiving ACLS. There was no report of epinephrine being administered in route.

I spoke to her husband who says that she has been really doing pretty well. She decided to donate blood a few days ago and yesterday began having her first menses since her baby was born. It was reportedly a very heavy menses. Accordingly she was very tired yesterday and today but blames it on the heavy bleeding and the fact that she has been getting very much sleep.

Her initial ECG here shows atrial fibrillation with some evidence of possible preexcitation in 1 of the QRS complexes. It is also possible that this was a fusion beat. She has since converted to normal sinus rhythm on amiodarone and her telemetry does not show any evidence of preexcitation. A twelve-lead ECG is pending at this time.

I personally performed a bedside echo. Her systolic function is severely depressed with an EF of 15 to 20%. The lateral wall seems to be moving okay but the septum and apex appear to be very hypokinetic. She has mild much regurgitation mild-to-moderate tricuspid regurgitation. Her PA pressures are not extremely elevated.

Allergies
Coded Allergies:
Unable to Obtain an Allergy History (Unverified, 6/11/19)
Assessment & Plan
Hospital Course

Ms. Firth is an unfortunate twenty-nine-year-old woman who suffered an out-of-hospital cardiac arrest. It is likely that she has postpartum cardiomyopathy leading to ventricular fibrillation.

Agree with amiodarone use for rhythm suppression for now.

Agree with hypothermia protocol to try to preserve cerebral function.

I spoke with the family and told him about the grave prognosis.

We will repeat a formal echocardiogram tomorrow morning.

We will see how her hemodynamics respond to sedation and cooling with an eye toward starting CHF regimen as soon as possible.

We will likely plan for left heart catheterization prior to discharge for the rare complication of coronary artery dissection in the postpartum period. She does have regional wall motion variation on echocardiogram.

Hayes, Kevin R. MD   Jun 11, 2019 18:15

About two and a half hours into their drive, John received a phone call from his aunt, Mary Jo Bain. Mary Jo is a retired registered nurse with a master's degree.

John answered, "Hello."

Mary Jo responded, "How are you and Andrea doing? I can't imagine the position you are in. Are you able to drive okay? I've been sitting here thinking about all of you and Christie."

John said, "Thanks for thinking of us. We are doing fine. The GPS has us getting to the hospital around 6:15 a.m. or so. We've got a long way to go. I don't know why this had to happen to Christie." His voice was breaking up and he was trying to hold back his tears. Mary Jo has always been very careful regarding medical advice and opinions. She asked if they had heard anything more from the doctors. John told her that they had not. John asked if what had happened to Christie would have something to do with giving birth two and a half months ago. Mary Jo said anything is possible. She also said it is highly unusual for this to happen. They talked a little longer and she wished them all the best and said she would be thinking about them. It was nice to have the phone call to break up the monotony of the road and to get them out of their heads for just a little while.

It was ten o'clock. Paula and Daniel were in the ICU waiting room with Brian. Christie could only have one visitor at a time. Paula took her turn to be with Christie. She walked into the ICU room. Her best friend was lying unconscious in the hospital bed. Christie didn't look like Christie. She had tubes in her arms and a breathing tube taped to her mouth. Her right temple was swollen and bruised, and she had dried blood on her face and in her hair. Paula was terrified as she looked at her friend and tears filled her eyes, and she thought to herself, *She looks like she has been hit by a baseball bat or as if she had been in a car accident. I can't imagine what Brian is feeling.* Paula looked at her friend and touched her hand and said, "Christie, it's Paula. I'm here for you and praying for you."

A little time had gone by and Paula returned to the ICU waiting room. She was scared. She knew Christie's parents were on their way and didn't know if they would get here in time and if Christie would make it through the night. She looked at Brian and then looked at Daniel, and she whispered in Daniel's ear, "I have no idea what he's going through, but he needs us." Paula then looked over at Brian. She didn't know if he was praying. In fact, she didn't know what Brian's religion was but she could feel that he was trying to pray as hard as he could. She had never seen a man so scared to lose the love of his life. She thought to herself that this is something you see in movies and you can kind of empathize with the character but when it's your best friend's husband sitting there worried whether she is going to wake up, that's another situation all together.

Brian looked at Paula and Daniel and said, "I don't know what I'm supposed to do with Westin."

Paula responded before she even realized what she was saying, "Just give him to me."

Daniel looked at Paula and asked, "Are you sure?"

Paula responded, "Give me the baby. Brian, your place is right here with Christie." Paula looked into Brian's eyes, and she could see that he was filled with gratitude and he knew that he didn't have to say a word.

Midnight. June 12, 2019. Andrea's birthday. John looked at his best friend and love as he drove down the road and she had her eyes closed. He said, "Happy Birthday, Honey, I love you." Andrea squeezed his hand.

Around 1:45 a.m. John had reached a point where he needed rest. Andrea was trying to rest but was having a hard time of it. John said, "Let's drive a little further and see if we can find a place to stop and rest for just a little bit."

Andrea said, "Do you want me to drive?"

John looked at Andrea and said, "We both need to rest and the only way we can do that is if we pull over." They were somewhere in Arkansas. John found a college campus to pull into and picked a parking lot to stop in. He found a light to park under and pulled into a parking spot. He shut the headlights off on the car and left it running so they would have air-conditioning and set his alarm for 2:45 a.m. It was 2:00 a.m. right now. He shut his eyes and went right to sleep.

Bzzz. Bzzz. John's eyes opened immediately. He woke up and shut off the alarm on his phone. Andrea woke as well and they both got their bearings. Andrea asked, "How are you doing?"

John responded, "I'm fine. That was just the amount of rest I needed."

They both knew better but they had to get to Christie. They headed on to Texarkana.

5

John and Andrea arrived on the campus of Christus St. Michael Hospital in Texarkana, Texas, around 7:15 a.m. They were familiar with the campus since Christie had given birth to Westin at this same hospital just a few months back. They headed to the intensive care unit.

John and Andrea approached the nurses' station in the ICU and identified themselves. Christie's room was right next to the nurses' station, and this location underscored how critical the situation was.

They were told that Christie was in an induced coma and was on a breathing machine. Although she could breathe on her own, the precaution was in place for the breathing assistance. The nurse said that Christie could hear them if they wanted to let her know they were there but she would not be able to respond.

John and Andrea walked into Christie's room. Even though they were given an idea of her situation it definitely hit them hard. Christie looked like she was a victim of an auto accident. She had tubes in her arms, she had a tube in her mouth. Her right eye around her temple was swollen and bruised. She had dried blood on the right side of her face. She had dry blood in her blond hair. Brian had been sleeping in a chair all night and woke up as John and Andrea came into the room. John grabbed his daughter's small left hand. In his mind he was seeing his little girl at the age of twelve. Andrea was by his side. Barely able to speak, but he knew he had to be strong for Christie, John said, "Christie, it's Dad. Your mom and I are right here. You've had an accident at work but you are going to be okay. Westin is good. Don't worry about him. Natalie is good too. Brian is right here with you and is fine. We just need you to be strong and to rest. If you understand me, just blink your eyes or squeeze my hand." Christie opened her eyes and blinked. She then squeezed John's hand. John, with tears rolling down his face said, "Did you see that? She understood me. She blinked her eyes and squeezed my hand." It was 7:30 a.m.

The doctors had decided that Christie's body temperature would need to be lowered in order to help her brain from swelling due to the impact her head had when it hit the safe in her office. Normal human body temperature is 98.6 degrees Fahrenheit. The plan was to lower Christie's body temperature to 91 degrees Fahrenheit. All of this taking place while she was in the induced coma.

It had been a long night for Brian. He asked if it was okay if he went home for a little bit to take care of his dogs and to check that his logging company was ready for the day in his absence. Andrea and John said, "Of course, go get done what needs to be done." They assured him they weren't going anywhere and if they heard anything, they would call him.

The lowering of the body temperature is a long process. They do it gradually as to not shock the patient during the process. It would be about a twelve-hour process followed by another twelve-hour process to warm Christie's body to its normal temperature.

6

There wasn't anything more John and Andrea could do for Christie at this time. Christie knew they were there, and she also knew she had to rest, and that is what she did. A little later in the morning John was introduced to the critical care chaplain, Kai Horn. She asked John what had happened with Christie and John told her what he knew. Kai is a Christian Methodist minister. She asked if she could visit Christie and say a prayer for her. John said of course.

When they walked into the room there were no signs of change. Andrea and Brian were there and John introduced them. Kai Horn introduced herself to Christie and said a prayer for her and her family. John thanked her. Kai smiled and said, "You are so welcome. God does the healing and we do the helping." Her visit could not have come at a better time for all.

This all didn't make sense. How does a very healthy twenty-nine-year-old woman go into cardiac arrest? The doctors mentioned that one possibility was that Christie had experienced peripartum cardiomyopathy (PPCM), also known as postpartum cardiomyopathy, which is an uncommon form of heart failure that happens during the last month of pregnancy or up to five months after giving birth. PPCM is a dilated form of the condition, which means the heart chambers enlarge and the muscle weakens.[2] The doctors told the family that this is very rare and happens to about 1200 women a year in the United States. This information gave the family a *source* of the problem and now they were ready to get after it and *fix it*.

---

[2]   Information courtesy of the American Heart Association.

There were so many people to contact or update that it was overwhelming. Andrea made the most of this time and started a private group Facebook page called "Christie's Journey." There are a lot of downsides to Facebook and there are a lot of times when social media in general has more cons than pros. This wasn't one of those times. It was wonderful! This allowed family and friends to be updated without the family having to text or call all of the time. Rather quickly the group grew to 254 members. Many friends and family left comments and prayers and the family found it quite therapeutic to read them.

Here are some of the comforting words and prayers that started showing up on the Christie's Journey Facebook Page:

> Keeping positive thoughts for regained strength.
>
> This is what the Lord says: I have heard your prayer and I will heal you.
>
> Whatever you ask for in prayer, believe that you have received and it will be yours. Mark 11:24
>
> Been praying for you sweet friend! You're amazing. Keep growing strong.
>
> Prayers for a speedy recovery and continued prayers for you and your family.
>
> Be strong in the Lord and in His mighty power. Ephesians 6:10
>
> Sending positive vibes and prayers.
>
> Prayer is powerful and this family was starting to witness that firsthand.

7

June 13, 2019

Christie's body temperature was warmed back to normal. The twenty-four-hour process, with the raising of her body temperature 0.23 degrees per hour, the second twelve hours, provided wonderful information that there was no brain damage.

Electrophysiology Prog Note
Subjective
General Information
Date and Time
Progress Note Documented on June 13, 2019 at 17:25 by the following provider: Odia O Russette, APRN
Admission Date/Time
Patient Admission date: June 11, 2019 at 18:08
Chief Complaint
VF arrest
Subjective
Ms. Firth remains in ICU. She is now extubated. She has been sleeping, but awakens easily. She is lethargic upon waking. She received Ativan IV. She does have some confusion. She denies any chest pain, shortness of breath, or nausea. She has developed a fever greater than 101F abd leukocytosis. Dr. White has ordered empiric antibiotics. She is in sinus tachycardia with a heart of 140 bpm on exam. Dr. Hayes has ordered metoprolol IV for rate control. Family remains at bedside.

Review of Systems
Unable to Obtain: Confused
Physical Exam
Vital Signs/I&Os

Date	Time	Temp	Pulse	Resp	B/P (MAP)	Pulse Ox	O2 Delivery O2 Flow Rate FiO2
6/13/19	17:20					98	Nasal Cannula 2.00 28
6/13/19	16:00		142	21	114/56 (75)		
					122/60 (80)		
6/13/19	15:00	100.9					

General Appearance: No apparent distress. Well-developed/nourished. **Lethargic**
Respiratory: No respiratory distress. No accessory muscle use, **Decreased Breath Sounds**
Extremities: No clubbing, no cyanosis, no edema
Psych/Mental Status: Anxious, confused
Neurologic: Cranial Nerves II–XII intact, no focal weakness
Skin: Other—Facial flushing noted
Data
Labs
6/13/19 09:00:
Blood Urea Nitrogen 4, Carbon Dioxide Level 19, Chloride Level 113, Creatinine 0.46, Glucose Level 103, Hematocrit 31.4, **Hemoglobin 10.8,** Platelet Count 192, Potassium Level 3.7, Sodium Level 140, **White Blood Count 12.7**
6/13/19 15:30:
Blood Urea Nitrogen 4, Carbon Dioxide Level 19, Chloride Level 111, Creatinine 0.56, Glucose Level 104, Hematocrit 32.4, Hemoglobin 10.9, Platelet Count 209, Potassium Level 3.8, Sodium Level 138, **White Blood Count 17.0**

CBC/BMP

6/13/19 09:00

12.7	10.8		140	113	4
192					103
	31.4			19	
		3.7	19	0.46	

6/13/19 15:30

17.0	**10.9**				**138**	**111**	**4**
	209						**104**
	32.4			**3.8**	**19**	**0.56**	

Cardiac Enzymes

Test   6/11/19
18:00
Troponin I 0.19 ng/ml
(0.00-0.04)

Cardiology

EKG

Sinus tachycardia 140 bpm

Normal interval and axis

T wave abnormality seen in the inferolateral pattern

Echo

Mitral Valve

Mild mitral regurgitation.

Aortic Valve

Mild AI.

Tricuspid Valve

Normal tricuspid valve structure and function.

Left Atrium

Left atrium size is normal.

Left ventricle

Mildly dilated left ventricle.

The ejection fraction was visually estimated at 40%.

Apical septal hypokinesis.

Abnormal left ventricular relaxation.

Right Atrium

Right atrium size is normal.

Right Ventricle

The right ventricle is normal in size, wall thickness, and contractility.

Pericardial Effusion

No evidence of pericardial effusion.

Pleural Effusion

No evidence of pleural effusion.

Miscellaneous
Medications
Current Medications Reviewed: Yes
Review
EKG Personally Reviewed, Labs Reviewed
Assessment & Plan
Hospital Course

Ms. Firth is an unfortunate twenty-nine-year-old woman who suffered an out-of-hospital cardiac arrest. It is likely that she has post-partum cardiomyopathy leading to ventricular fibrillation.

Agree with amiodarone use for rhythm suppression for now.

Agree with hypothermia protocol to try to preserve cerebral function.

I spoke with the family and told him about the grave prognosis.

We will repeat a formal echocardiogram tomorrow morning.

We will see how her hemodynamics respond to sedation and cooling with an eye toward starting CHF regimen as soon as possible.

We will likely plan for left heart catheterization prior to discharge for the rare complication of coronary artery dissection in the postpartum period. She does have regional wall motion variation on echocardiogram.

6/13/19

Ms. Firth remains in the ICU. Hypothermia protocol completed. She is awake and extubated. Sinus tachycardia etiology uncertain and persists despite improvement of temperature. We will likely consider ICD for secondary prevention following VF arrest. We will add a UA and blood cultures for fever and leukocytosis.

We will attempt rate control with oral dosing of metoprolol.
Impression:

1. VF Arrest
2. Cardiomyopathy, like postpartum
3. Sinus tachycardia
4. Fever, post arrest
5. Leukocytosis

—Add UA and blood cultures prior to antibiotics
—Add metoprolol oral dosing for rate control
—Continue to monitor. Will increase metoprolol dosing to her tolerance.

VTE Assessment
Risk for VTE (Select based on: Moderate)
VTE Mechanical Prophylaxis: Compression Device…—Knee High
Russette, Odia O APRN   June 13, 2019 17:33

—REPORT ADDENDUM—
Addendum: Hayes, Kevin R MD on 6/13/19 @ 22:31
    Ms. Firth was independently interviewed and examined. Her case was discussed with Odia Russette, APRN. Happily, she is waking up and following commands. Her systolic function has improved from initial bedside evaluation. Her estimated EF is 40%. She does have apical hypokinesis. Plan for coronary CTA tomorrow a.m. if her rates are better controlled. Likely plan for ICD for secondary prevention of sudden cardiac death prior to discharge. Will follow up in the a.m.

6/13/19 2234—Electronically signed by Kevin R Hayes MD
    At 1:39 a.m. John received a text from his brother Joe, it read: "How's it going?" John didn't see the text right away and responded at 3:37 a.m. "Her temp has gone up one degree. It's a slow process. I just spoke to her and she responded by blinking. I told her to blink her eyes if she understood and she did! She did this more than once."
    Christie's friend, April Thompson, had spent most of the night at the hospital and was with Andrea when Christie was becoming more alert. John and Brian were in the waiting room in order to allow less stimulation and distractions so that Christie could rest.
    Dr. White, the intensive care unit doctor, announced to Andrea and April that he would be starting a two-hour breathing treatment for Christie and if all goes well, the breathing tube could be removed. When the doctor left the room, Christie started to communicate with her mother and April. She was desperately trying to

ask something and moved her hand. Andrea told her to relax as best as she could and that the doctors would be removing the tube soon. Christie motioned her hand again. This time with a looping motion indicating that she wanted to write. Andrea got her a sheet of paper on a clipboard and handed it to her.

Christie wrote in cursive: "What's wrong with me? Where is Westin?"

Andrea responded, "You fell at work. You have had some sort of heart issue. Westin is fine and he is with Miss Paula."

Christie gave Andrea the strangest look. Andrea said, "We wouldn't lie. He is fine and she will bring him up later."

Andrea asked Christie, "Are you okay if April stays here with you while I go get Brian?"

Christie nodded.

Andrea entered the waiting room anxiously and with a smile. She handed the clipboard to Brian and John looked over Brian's shoulder at it. Andrea said, "She's awake and she's writing." Brian and John read what she had written. Brian started writing back to her to answer her questions. Andrea and John said together, "Brian, you can go talk to her." Brian smiled and away they all went to be with Christie.

The three got back to the room and Brian said, "Christie, I'm here." Christie opened her eyes and gave a look of relief to see Brian. John looked at his daughter and told her that she was going to be okay and to listen to the doctors and nurses so she could get better faster. April held her friend's hand. This was progress, but there was still a long way to travel on this journey.

At 9:01 a.m. John texted Joe and said: "Getting lots of good signs. She is responding with hand squeezes and head nods and eye blinks. She even gestured that she wants to write. It's a great day! Please share with mom and Joni." Joe smiled on his end and replied, "That's great, I will share." John thanked his brother.

Later that day at 1:06 p.m. John sent another text to Joe: "No brain damage! Woohoo!!!"

Joe responded, "Awesome."

John replied, "It's so awesome!"

Joe asked, *"How is her heart?"*

John typed back to his brother, "So far so good. Should be an issue that can be handled with medication. Will know more later. She is at 36.8 degrees Celsius. As soon as she gets to 37 degrees, they will do a CPAP test to check her breathing. All goes good, they will remove the tube. So far things appear to being all going in the right direction."

Joe replied back to his brother, "Maybe there is a god."

John quickly replied back, "Joe, there is. And I am thankful! I'm the richest man in the world! I'm getting my daughter back!"

Joe responded, "And very blessed."

John typed back, "Yep!"

Christie experienced success with the two-hour breathing treatment and the tube was removed from her throat. All were relieved. Christie could now talk. Her throat was sore from having the air constantly moving down her throat. She was able to have ice chips but they didn't taste right to her. This was a sensation that the nurses assured her would go away soon.

Christie had no memory of what had happened to her the past couple of days. In fact, she was confused. She was mixing her current stay in the hospital to when she gave birth to Westin back in March. Christie said to John, "Dad, don't you remember we all stopped at Denny's for breakfast before we came here?"

John smiled, "Honey, I do remember that but that was March 28 and Westin was born on the 29. This is June 13."

Christie looked at her dad and shook her head in disbelief as she tried to piece everything together. Christie said to John, "I can't afford to be in a hospital."

John held his daughter's hand and said, "Don't worry about that. It'll be okay."

She closed her eyes. She now was experiencing a fever.

John sent another text to his brother at 3:06 p.m.; "They have removed the breathing tube. She is resting comfortably. They don't want her to talk for the next couple of hours. She has a notepad to write on when she is ready. She is sleeping now."

Joe responded back to his brother, "Amazing news very happy need a Kleenex."

John replied back to his brother with a smiley face emoticon, "Our nerves are shot but very happy."

Joe typed back, "I can't imagine but it's a huge relief for everyone."

John responded, "Yes!"

Christie rested most of the day. In the afternoon, Andrea was sitting next to Christie's bed. Brian and John had stepped out for a while to get something to eat. They would bring back something for Andrea. Christie opened her eyes and looked around and then looked at Andrea and said, "Mom, I heard Aunt Beth's voice." All sorts of emotions welled up inside of Andrea. She quickly responded to her daughter, "Oh, that's nice." Christie closed her eyes again. Andrea didn't know if at this point if Christie remembered that Beth had died or if Christie actually did hear her aunt's heavenly voice. Andrea also wondered if Beth had to leave us in order for Christie to stay with us.

John texted his brother Joe a lot today. At 5:44 p.m., he texted Joe with the following: "Just got news she will need a defibrillator put in before she goes home."

Joe texted back, "Inside of her to monitor and give her a shock if needed?"

John typed back, "Yes."

Joe replied, *"How is her fever?"*

John responded, "She has a fever. They are just now getting some ice in a bag to put on her chest to help cool her down."

Joe replied, "Hopefully that helps."

John told his brother, "They have a fan blowing on her too."

Entries of support continued to come on Christie's Journey's Facebook Page. Here is a sample:

> Dear God, Touch, heal, restore, amend, redeem, awaken, hold, breathe, sing, speak! We invite you to come and be Lord in this situation. We open our hearts, our minds, our hands and welcome your restoring power. May this sickness

end and may your healing begin. In Jesus name, Amen.

I lift up my eyes to the hills. From where does my help come? My help comes from the Lord, who made heaven and earth. Psalm 121:1–2 ESV

Prayers for you my sweet friend! You got this!

Keep fighting Christie!

Praying for full recovery

My prayers are with you and your family.

Praying for you girl be strong.

The Lord has a purpose for you to fulfill, the power to equip you, and the strength to uphold you.

Be strong in the Lord and in His mighty power. Ephesians 6:10

Keeping you all in my thoughts and prayers!

Continuing to pray for Christie and the whole family.

Been praying hard for y 'all.

Good start still send prayers.

Praying for God's strength and peace over your family and Christie as her temp is raised. Praying for an excellent outcome and for her recovery, healing and restoration. Sending our love & hugs.

Oh my goodness, so sorry to hear everything that is going on Andy. Praying for you all. Christie is strong and can get through this!!! Anxious to hear updates over the next few days.

Awesome! Keep those prayers coming!!

And the prayers continued.

8

June 14, 2019

Andrea entered the following information into the Christie's Journey Facebook page: "She has been fighting a fever since 3:30 pm Thursday afternoon. Just had a sponge bath and that seemed to help. Praying for continued miracles on Friday. Her heart is weakened and we will be working with cardiologist on her options. Keep those prayers coming."

John was in Christie's ICU room along with Christie and Brian's friends, James and April Thompson. They were having a good visit and Christie was still trying to piece the past few days together in her memory. Andrea and Brian were resting in the waiting room. Andrea noticed two police officers walking through the waiting room and heading for the intensive care unit. She thought that was interesting and sent John a text that policemen were heading toward the ICU. John didn't think much about the text and went on visiting with the others.

A few minutes later, two police officers knocked on the door and entered Christie's room. Police Captain Welch introduced himself along with the other officer with him, Officer Michael Wade. Captain Welch started talking and said that he and Officer Wade were there to see how Christie was doing. Christie responded, "I am doing okay. They aren't sure why this happened to me. I don't remember anything that happened that day." Captain Welch responded that was probably to be expected and probably part of the healing process.

He then went on to mention that Officer Wade was the first, first responder on the scene and had started CPR.

Things started clicking very quickly for John at this point and he turned toward Officer Wade. Tears were welling up in John's eyes and he said, "Sir, thank you. Thank you for giving my daughter a chance. I don't know what else to say. I'm giving you a hug!" John hugged Officer Wade and thanked him again.

John sent a text to Andrea, "Come to Christie's room. You need to meet someone." Andrea and Brian made it to Christie's room. They were quite surprised to see the policemen in there. John said to them, "This is Captain Welch and Officer Michael Wade. Officer Wade performed CPR on Christie until the ambulance got there. He helped save her life!" Brian shook hands with both men.

John said to Brian, "Give this man a hug!" Brian was happy to do so. John introduced Andrea and she hugged Officer Wade as well. John then took out his iPhone and showed the police officers a picture of Christie with her baby boy Westin. Christie was somewhat overwhelmed by the meeting and was also grateful to Officer Wade. Christie shook hands with both men and hugged Officer Wade. The two men also shook hands with April and James and prepared to head back to the Red River Army Depot in Hooks, Texas. John looked at Officer Michael Wade and said, "Sir, if you ever thought you were in the wrong profession or had made the wrong career choice, please know that I believe you made the right decision." Officer Wade smiled and they shook hands one more time, then he departed with his captain.

April and James said their well-wishes and headed on their way promising to come back soon. The family started to discuss how *lucky*, *fortunate*, and *blessed* they were, that if this had to happen to Christie that it is good it happened where and when it did. Had this happened after work, when Christie was driving home, what might have happened to her or others? Had this happened at home when she would have been there alone with baby Westin, she wouldn't be here now. John said, "God has a plan and he has you in it, Christie. He has lined up angels this whole way that have helped you. We're going to get through this okay. I know it."

Christie had a visit that afternoon from a coworker of hers that she hardly knew, since she started shortly before Christie left for maternity leave. The visitor was Dean Renae McCray. She was the first one to start CPR on Christie. She was so relieved to see that Christie was doing much better than the last time she saw her. They talked a little and Dean mentioned that her older brother was friends with Brian while growing up in New Boston and all mentioned how life takes us on different paths and turns. She hadn't seen Brian since they were kids. None of them would have ever guessed that they would have been brought together again this way. Before Dean left, she received a big hug and thanks from John, Andrea, and Brian. Dean held Christie's hand, and Christie looked at Dean and said, "Thank you." The ladies hugged and Dean headed for home.

Andrea updated the Christie's Journey Facebook page:

> The cardiologist wants heart rate to stable a bit more before doing a CT scan. So, they should be doing that in the next few days. He thinks the best option is for a defibrillator which would be done before we leave. He was thrilled to see her talking. From what the Red River Police said this morning we are so lucky, we r just battling white blood count at the moment. Keep the prayers coming. Thank you for everyone's thoughts and prayers.

Later that evening, John and Andrea received a text from their son, Sean. The time was 10:49 p.m. The text read, "Pulling up now." They were both very thankful that Sean made it to Texarkana safely and would be with them. Having Sean there made the family stronger. Sean had helped his parents already by securing a hotel room for them near the hospital. John and Andrea were able to take advantage of it and get some rest, although not more than two or three hours at a time, since they wanted to be with Christie as much as possible. Brian stayed in Christie's room with her throughout. John and Andrea offered him their hotel room but he wanted to be with Christie.

John met Sean in the emergency room and walked him up to Christie's room. Andrea gave Sean a big hug and then Sean looked at his sister. Christie was sleeping and Sean told her he was there. Christie nodded her head. She was very tired and still fighting the fever. Andrea thanked Sean for the hotel room and encouraged him to use it now to get rest after his long drive. Sean stayed a while and then took his dad with him. Both men did not want to leave but knew they needed to get rest in order to be there fully for Christie.

9

June 15, 2019

It has been an up-and-down roller-coaster ride for Christie and her family. She has fought fevers and infection. Her white blood cells are starting to increase.

Dr. White stopped into Christie's room and gave her an assessment. As soon as the infection is under control, she would have a cardiology test to see what is going on with her heart and what the next steps will be. There is a good chance that Christie will have to have a defibrillator installed into her body. For the moment though, Dr. White suggested she go for a walk. This is the first time that she has walked since she had the cardiac arrest. With the aid of a nurse, Christie walked around the entire intensive care unit inner walls two full laps. She was tired afterward but gave a smile after her accomplishment and that made her family very happy.

Sean asked Christie, "Christie, do you remember talking to me and texting me on Tuesday about Mom's gift for her birthday and Dad's gift for Father's Day?"

Christie responded with a confused look on her face and her head motioning no. Christie replied, "I don't remember that, Sean."

Sean said, "It's okay. You've been through a lot and it will come back to you when it's time to." Sean smiled at his sister assuredly.

John, Andrea, and Sean convinced Brian that he should go to the hotel and stretch out on a real bed and get some rest and a shower. He needs to take care of himself so that he can be there for Christie and his kids. Brian accepted the offer, kissed Christie goodbye, and went to get some much-needed rest. Sean took his mother to go get some lunch and to give her a break from the hospital room for a little while.

A nurse came into Christie's room shortly after everyone had departed. She said she was there to wash Christie's hair. Christie welcomed that very much. She still had dried blood in her hair and it wasn't a comfortable feeling. The nurse was very careful and did a wonderful job cleaning her up. John thanked her for taking care of his daughter and showed the nurse a picture of Christie with Natalie and Westin. He said, "This is what she really looks like. Thanks for helping her get back to a more 'normal' feeling."

The nurse smiled and responded, "You're welcome. What little cutie pies." She turned to Christie and said, "If you need anything, honey, just push that button and I'll be on my way."

Christie thanked her.

John took this moment to ask the nurse a question. "Excuse me, ma'am, do you see those splotches on Christie? There on her arm and around her collarbone?"

The nurse said, "Yes, I don't know what would cause that."

John asked, "Is that pooling?" This is a term he learned when Andrea's parents were in hospice. It is a sign that the person is in the dying process. The nurse quickly responded, "No, that isn't pooling. We will have the doctor take a look at it though." John was relieved to hear that at least it wasn't pooling.

At 12:18 p.m. John updated Joe via text: "She's doing pretty darned good! She has gone for a walk. Had some breakfast. Done well with observations from the swallowing specialist. Gone to the bathroom twice and has had breathing treatment twice now. She now will be on a regular diet! They have also put in for a transfer out of ICU! Dr. White came in and listened to her lungs. Told her she is doing remarkably well and because of that he will have to break up with her and move her out of ICU. She is having lunch now."

Joe responded to his brother, "That's great news!"

John replied, "Yes!"

Christie received several visits from friends and coworkers throughout the day. All were welcomed and therapeutic but none as welcomed and therapeutic as seeing Natalie and Westin. Christie's best friend, Paula Simmons, had been watching the children overnights while their good friend, Rhonda Stone, had been watching them during the day. Paula brought the children to the hospital to be reunited with their mother. "Knock, knock. Are you up for some visitors?" Christie, Brian, Andrea, and John looked toward the door. It was Miss Paula with the kids. All were excited and Christie responded with a big smile and her arms outreached, "Yes I am!" Natalie approached her mom and Christie said, "Hi, Honey, I'm so glad to see you." Christie and Natalie hugged and Natalie sat next to Christie in her bed. Everyone present could see the relief in Natalie's face and demeanor. Christie looked at Natalie with a big smile on her face and said, "You got your cast off! It's nice to see all of your arm again." Natalie smiled and moved her arm around to show her mom that it was all good again.

Andrea gave Paula a big hug and started doting over Westin who was still in his stroller. Westin started fussing like babies do and Andrea, "Gigi," couldn't get him to settle down. She brought Westin to Christie's bed and placed him on Christie. Christie said, "What's wrong with my little man?" She was holding him and as she spoke and held him, he immediately settled right down. Westin knows his momma and it was evident they both needed this reunion. Christie asked Paula, "How is he doing for you?"

Paula smiled and said, "He is absolutely perfect." Paula marveled at how Westin immediately recognized Christie and how content he was with her. Paula also marveled at how Christie now looked like Christie again. Brian had a calming presence about him now and things were much better than a few nights ago when Paula was worried whether Christie would make it through the night. God is good.

Paula's husband, Daniel, had worked with Brian at the Red River Army Depot. They had become good friends and it was very easy for Christie and Paula to become best of friends, and the couples got together on a regular basis. Daniel and Paula have two children,

Caleb and Abbi. Caleb is eight and Abbi is seven. Paula worked at the Red River Credit Union, and she made Christie aware of an opening there and Christie applied. Once Christie was hired, the two ladies saw each other every day at work and spent a lot of time together which developed into their strong relationship.

10

June 16, 2019

Andrea posted onto the Christie's Journey Facebook page:

> Day 6 and she feels like she has been hit by
> a truck. So the good meds are out of her system.
> She hasn't had a blood culture done yet to see if
> her numbers have gone down. Fingers crossed.
> We r hoping she can have heart test done on
> Monday.

Lora Bain was attending church service, like most Sundays at Eicher Emmanuel Mennonite Church, in Wayland, Iowa. Pastor Dave Schooley proceeded with his sermon: "I wish we could go around the room today and share, one with another, when you have been most moved to praise God. Surely, what brings us to praise the Lord varies depending on circumstances and our own mental and emotional state of well-being. We are going to talk about praise today and the conversation starter for our praise discussion is the 113th Psalm. You heard it already and you will hear it again. But first this from A.W. Tozer, 'In almost everything that touches our everyday life on earth, God is pleased when we're pleased. He wills that we be as free as birds to soar and sing our maker's praise without anxiety.' The Psalms contain praise and we should hear this Psalm again.

Praise the LORD!
Praise, O servants of the LORD,
    praise the name of the LORD!
Blessed be the name of the LORD
    from this time forth and forevermore!
From the rising of the sun to its setting,
    the name of the LORD is to be praised!
The LORD is high above all nations,
    and his glory above the heavens!
Who is like the LORD our God,
    who is seated on high,
who looks far down
    on the heavens and the earth? He raises the
    poor from the dust
    and lifts the needy from the ash heap,
to make them sit with princes,
    with the princes of his people.
He gives the barren woman a home,
making her the joyous mother of children.
Praise the LORD!" (Ps. 113:1–9)

We should grasp, we should contemplate what it is that moves us to praise him! But, not everything in our experience moves us to praise. Even in this great Psalm of praise we read in verse 7 that he raises the poor from the dust and lifts the needy from the ash heap. So those being raised and lifted have experienced difficulty in life. This Psalm is actually trying to describe the worst difficulty. Some translations might use dung heap rather than ash heap. There were those who scavenged in refuse, the dump, just outside the city gates. These were the forgotten ones, the lowest of the low and the Psalmist recognizes that our God raises and lifts to the place of princes.

Actually, their circumstances may not have changed but their standing in God's eyes should change us. Our great God sees each one with equal value whether they praise him or not, he loves each one because he is love. He can do no other because it would violate who he is not to love. It is a great reason to praise.

When we see miracles of transformation; changed hearts, lives, and values we have reason to praise. From time to time we may see miracles of provision, or healing. You recall the story of the missionary family receiving a quilt and later discovering $300 pinned to that quilt. Paul Ramseyer stage 4 stomach cancer anointed with oil.

Then Lora became quite surprised when Pastor Dave started discussing her great niece Christie and a picture of Christie with Westin, that she had shared earlier with the pastor, appeared on the big screen at the front of the sanctuary. Pastor Dave continued, "Praise for regaining health, praise for mother and child to be reunited, and praise for medical personnel. Can your praise continue? If you know, beyond a shadow of a doubt, that all those things the Apostle Paul spoke of last week, "Neither death nor life, nor angels nor rulers, nor things present nor things to come, nor powers, nor height nor depth, nor anything else in all creation, will be able to separate us from the love of God in Christ Jesus our Lord."

Then you will praise him as he holds your very life in his hands you will praise him "Go forth today, by the help of God's Spirit, vowing and declaring that in life—-come poverty, come wealth, in death—come pain or come what may, you are and ever must be the Lord's. For this is written on your heart, 'We love Him because He first loved us'" (Charles H. Spurgeon).

There are many questions in life. What moves you to praise God, how do you see him raise and lift one from the ash heap, and, finally, can your praise continue are all questions that speak to us of how we see and perceive the love of God and what our love looks like. Not all Psalms are of praise. There is a place for lament as well and in two weeks we will try another Psalm. Let us pray, we praise the one true God, we sing of your majesty, we sing of your glory, we tell of your goodness to each one of us. Accept our praise oh Lord as we say thank you for your boundless love and may we search for ways to say we love you. As Spurgeon said, "Go forth today because it is written on your heart, 'We love him because he first loved us!'"[3]

---

[3] Sermon information provided by Pastor Dave Schooley's personal notes

Christie had several well-wishers stop by today. All were shocked at what had happened and relieved to see and be with her in person. Christie was glad to see everyone but she was also weak and tired. Andrea did a good job of making sure visits weren't too long.

When the two were alone, Christie asked Andrea, "Mom, when can I see Natalie and Westin?" Andrea grew concerned since Paula had just brought the kids to visit the day before. Andrea responded to Christie, "Honey, you have seen them. Paula brought them here to you just yesterday." Christie looked at her mother with a confused look and shook her head. Andrea handed Christie her phone and showed the worried young mother some pictures that were taken of her and the kids yesterday. Christie looked at the pictures and relaxed.

She said to Andrea, "I'm just so tired."

Andrea said, "I know you are, sweetie. You've been through a lot. Just close your eyes and get some sleep."

Christie listened to her mother.

It was Father's Day. John was thinking and thanking God that his daughter was still with us. It was the best gift he could ever have. He was thankful and grateful. Miss Paula brought Natalie and Westin to the hospital that afternoon so the family could be together. All the family gathered around Christie's bed with Christie holding Westin and Natalie sitting next to them for a family picture. John posted it so all the friends and family could see and titled the picture, "Best Father's Day Ever!"

John walked down to Paula's car carrying Westin in his car seat along with Paula and Natalie. Outside in the parking lot, John helped get Westin's car seat snapped into its base. "Paula, thank you so much for all that you are doing for Christie and our family. We all truly appreciate it."

Paula smiled. "Christie is my best friend, Mr. John. I want to help as much as I can."

John smiled and handed Paula a one hundred dollar bill. Paula looked at the money and said, "I can't take this. We don't need it. We're fine."

John said, "I know that. I want you to use this for Westin's diapers or formula or anything else he might need. I know it won't go very far. I don't have much cash on me at the moment. Please use this."

Paula thanked John and promised that she would. He gave Westin a kiss and told him to be a good boy and then went around to the other side of the car to get a hug from Natalie. John looked at his granddaughter, she was buckled in. He said, "Now you keep being a good girl and help Ms. Paula. Okay?"

Natalie looked at her Papa John and said, "I will, Papa, I love you."

John smiled, "I love you too, young lady!"

11

June 17, 2019

Paula had been on Facebook and noticed a post from the Red River Army Depot. It read as follows: "Red River Army Depot, June 17, 2019, For Red River Police Officer Michael Wade, a recent evening patrol on TexAmericas Center led to the officer helping save the life of a Red River Federal Credit Union employee. Last Tuesday, Officer Wade was waved down by the supervisor of the Red River Federal Credit Union on TexAmericas Center property to report an emergency medical situation involving one of their employees. On arrival at the Credit Union, Officer Wade was met with a patient in full cardiac arrest. Officer Wade immediately called for assistance and began performing CPR on the victim until paramedics arrived on the scene. "If it wasn't for Officer Wade's quick actions and continued support, we would have likely lost this patient," said Brett Wilson, RRAD firefighter/paramedic. Officer Wade is pictured receiving a Commander's Coin from COL York for his heroic and life-saving actions. Christie's family was proud of the recognition that Officer Wade received and shared this post with all on the Christie's Journey Facebook Page as well as their own personal Facebook pages.

All things considered; Christie was doing well. Dr. Hayes decided that she would have the test on her heart tomorrow. The family hoped for answers and good news regarding her future treatment. Andrea asked Dr. Hayes about the splotches on Christie. He looked them over but really didn't have an explanation for them and didn't seem worried about them. That made Andrea feel a little better.

Christie had a visit from a friend of hers, Brandy Green. Brandy is a very talented young lady, and she presented a gift to Christie. "I wanted to do something for you and this is what I came up with." Brandy pulled a navy-blue T-shirt out of her bag. It had a pink heartbeat symbol like you would see on a heart monitor with a shape of a heart in between the monitor lines. Below that in white lettering it read, And The Beat Goes On…below that a few lines in white letters, #OneToughMama. Christie loved it! It made her feel good and summed up her current situation very well.

12

June 18, 2019

Brian and Andrea had spent the night with Christie. There was no way either of them would not be there when it was time for her heart test. It was 7:30 a.m. The nurse came in to get Christie. "Good morning, Christie, I'm here to take you for your heart cath (cardiac catheterization)."

Christie smiled and said, "Hi, okay."

Brian kissed Christie and wished her good luck. Andrea hugged her daughter and told her it would be okay. Cardiac catheterization is a procedure used to diagnose and treat certain cardiovascular conditions. During cardiac catheterization, a long thin tube called a catheter is inserted in an artery or vein in your groin, neck, or arm and threaded through your blood vessels to your heart.[4] John and Sean had gone back to the hotel to sleep and shower. At 9:18 a.m. Andrea texted John and said, "Nurse said she should be back to room in a few minutes and doctor will be up."

John told Sean what his mom had sent in the text.

Sean said, "I guess we better get moving then."

John responded, "Yes, we better."

About two minutes later, Christie, in her bed, arrived back in her room being pushed by the nurse and accompanied by Dr. Kevin Hayes. Christie had tears rolling down her face and said to Andrea, "Mom, it's not good." Dr. Hayes interjected what the test had found,

---

[4] Information courtesy of Mayo Clinic.

57

"It appears that Christie was born with a birth defect in her heart. Her pulmonary artery is connected to the wrong side of the heart. Instead of bringing the freshest and oxygenated blood to her heart, it passes through her body first and then what is left goes into her heart. She is going to have to have surgery right away, and I'm going to start contacting my colleagues at Mayo, Little Rock and Cleveland so that we can take care of this the best way for Christie." Dr. Hayes excused himself, and Andrea and Brian were stunned. Andrea looked at Christie. She had been holding her hand since she got back. Andrea said to Christie, "Christie, when was the last time you didn't hit a challenge head on?" Christie shook her head and Andrea said, "We'll get through this."

Andrea sent a follow-up text to John, "Take an Uber now," followed by an immediate text, "Sounds like open heart."

John replied, "What?"

Andrea followed up with another text, "In Little Rock Children's hospital."

John was confused. He responded, "You don't make sense!" John shared with Sean what Andrea had sent. John said, "We have to roll now. Let's get going!" The two men headed to reunite with their family in the ICU.

Shortly after John and Sean had arrived in Christie's room, Dr. White came in. He smiled at everyone and asked Christie how she was doing. Christie responded, "I don't understand how this could happen."

Dr. White said to Christie, "You are a miracle. Most people who have this condition don't make it past their teen years because they don't know about it and when they overexert themselves in sports, many have died on the playing field because of it being an unknown untreated condition."

John said out loud, "Christie played sports her whole life growing up. Her mother and I coached several of her teams. Are you saying it's a miracle she has lived this long?!"

Dr. White responded, "Yes. From doing all the *normal* things people do in their lives and plus just having a baby and going through the delivery process, she is very fortunate she didn't pass away then or while going through child birth." John, like everyone else in the room, was stunned.

Christie's heart's ejection fraction measurement was measured at 20. Ejection fraction (EF) is a measurement expressed as a percentage of how much blood the left ventricle pumps out with each contraction. An ejection fraction of 60 percent means that 60 percent of the total amount of blood in the left ventricle is pushed out with each heartbeat. A normal heart's ejection fraction may be between 50 and 70 percent. An ejection fraction measurement under 40 percent may be evidence of heart failure or cardiomyopathy. Cardiomyopathy refers to diseases of the heart muscle. These diseases have many causes, signs, and symptoms as well as treatments. In most cases, cardiomyopathy causes the heart muscle to become enlarged, thick, or rigid. In rare instances, diseased heart muscle tissue is replaced with scar tissue. An EF from 41 to 49 percent may be considered "borderline." It does not always indicate that a person is developing heart failure. Instead, it may indicate damage, perhaps from a previous heart attack. In severe cases, ejection fraction can be very low.[5] With Christie's heart's EF at 20, her medical team knew they had to act fast.

Andrea posted on Christie's Journey Facebook page: "No visitors today, please." The family needed to put a game plan in place, led by Dr. Hayes and now that they knew what the problem was it was time to get busy on finding a solution and getting Christie better.

Dr. Kevin R Hayes entered the following information on the Cardiology Cath Proc Note;

Cardiology Cath Proc Note
Procedure
Date/Time:
Date/Time: Jun 18, 2019 at 17:40
Performed by:
Kevin R. Hayes, MD
Indications:
Cardiac Catheterization Procedure Report Summary
Primary Indication

---

[5] Information courtesy of www.heart.org.

Out-of-hospital cardiac arrest, congestive heart failure
Procedures
Left heart cath + ventriculogram + coronary angiography (93458)

Under my direct supervision, sedation was provided by the cath lab nurse and the patient was independently monitored. A total of 1.5 mg of Versed and 75 mcg of Fentanyl was administered for a total sedation time of 58 min.

Vascular Access
Location: right radial artery, right femoral vein
Sheath: 6Fr (right radial), 6FR right femoral vein
Disposition (end of case): radial—TR band; femoral—hemostasis with manual pressure
Catheters
Diagnostic: TIGR, JR4, Pigtail
Diagnostic Findings
Hemodynamics (mm Hg)
Aorta: 115/81, mean 96
LV: 123/8. EDP 22
Pulmonary artery: 39/18, mean 28
Right ventricle: 47/7, EDP 14
Right atrium: Mean 10

Oxygen saturations were performed from the carina of the pulmonary artery, proximal pulmonary artery, right ventricle, and right atrium. The oxygen saturations were all around 70%. There was no step-up identified.

Coronary arteries:
Left main accessed and angiography was performed in multiple views: Large caliber vessel, the left main coronary artery had an anomalous takeoff from the base of the pulmonary artery, contrast filled from the right coronary artery.

LAD accessed and angiography was performed in multiple views: Large caliber, filled via the right coronary artery.

LCx accessed and angiography was performed in multiple views: Large caliber, filled via the right coronary artery.

RCA accessed and angiography was performed in multiple views: Large caliber, fills the entire left circulation via collaterals. No significant disease.

Coronary circulation dominance: Right

Initially we are unable to find the left main coronary artery. Aortography was performed showing no evidence of left main filling.

A pigtail catheter was then inserted into the pulmonary artery via femoral vein approach. Pulmonary arteriography was performed showing the branch of the left main coming off the pulmonary artery just superior to the pulmonic valve.

Left ventriculography

EF 45–50%

Adverse Events

None

Contrast Total

250 ml

Fluoroscopy

8.8 min

Impressions

Nonobstructive coronary disease

Anomalous coronary takeoff of the left main from the pulmonary artery leading to sudden cardiac death

Mild LV systolic dysfunction

Recommendations

Risk factor modification

Routine post-cath care with a TR band

I have spoken with Cleveland Clinic who has accepted her in transfer for corrective surgery for the anomalous left main coronary artery.

Hayes, Kevin R. MD   June 18, 2019 17:47

13

After lots of praying and lots of discussion, the decision was made that Christie would have to have open-heart surgery to correct the problem. Throughout the process, discussion included everything from open-heart surgery to heart replacement. These were very scary times for Christie and her family and friends. Dr. Hayes has good colleagues in Cleveland, Ohio, at the world-renowned hospital, the Cleveland Clinic. He made arrangements for Christie's arrival and also arranged for a medical plane to transport Christie and Brian to Cleveland from the Texarkana Airport.

The family had been waiting all afternoon in anticipation of Christie and Brian's departure. Paula brought Westin and Natalie to the hospital so they could have some time with their mother. Christie held Westin in her bed and played with him and cuddled with him. The little baby knew he was with his momma and seemed very content. Natalie sat close to Christie on her bed and told her momma that she hoped she would be okay. Christie smiled at Natalie and gave her hand a reassuring squeeze, "I'm going to be okay, Honey, and I'll be home soon." Natalie smiled. This was a lot for a seven-year-old to take in.

Evening came, and Christie and Brian were still at the hospital in Texarkana. Paula took the children back to her place. As soon as it seemed nothing was going to happen, the team responsible for getting Christie to her awaiting medical airplane transport arrived. It was time to go. John and Andrea said their goodbyes to Christie and Brian and also assured them they would see them the next day in

Cleveland. Sean had left for Iowa the day before to get back to work for at least a day or so.

Christie was loaded in an ambulance and Brian accompanied her. The next stop was the Texarkana Airport. When they arrived at the airport the ambulance was allowed to drive onto the tarmac and close to the awaiting medical transport plane. The plane was staffed with a pilot, doctor, and nurse. Christie's cart was loaded onto the center of the plane. There was a jump seat for the doctor, nurse, and Brian. Next stop—Cleveland, Ohio.

14

Andrea made the following entry onto the Christie's Journey Facebook Page: "Christie is now in Cleveland Clinic in Cleveland, OH at one of the best Heart Clinics in the world. Brian is with her and John and I are on the way."

John posted the following: "Well, my daughter, Christie Firth, is in need of open-heart surgery. She is now at the Cleveland Clinic in Cleveland, Ohio, with her husband, Brian Firth. Andy Bain and I are on our way there from Texarkana. Pictured here with Christie and her son Westin, is good friend Paula Flournoy Simmons. She has been taking care of Westin overnights and the weekends. Good friend, Rhonda Stone, is taking care of him during the day. Please pray or keep praying for Christie and all of us. So far, she has been a miracle in so many ways!"

Back in Texas, Paula had recently started reattending her hometown church, Westside Missionary Baptist Church, in New Boston. She knew that if she hadn't been back to her church that she would not be able to handle mentally going through this right now. Shortly after Paula had first received the information that Christie was in trouble, she sent a group text to her pastor, the song leader, and a few of the Sunday School teachers that are a huge part of her support group, and they immediately started sending prayers right up. The congregation had been conducting prayer services for Christie and Westin. Paula could feel their prayers touching her and touching

Christie and her family. She continued to pray for a full recovery for Christie.

At 11:44 a.m. John sent a text to Christie, "We are at the Dallas airport. How are you doing?"

Christie texted back to her dad, "Doing good, they are talking about doing another cath lab like they did yesterday. And then tomorrow an MRI scan. They are thinking they may do the open-heart surgery and defibrillator."

John asked back, "When are they thinking?"

Christie told her dad, "They have to do those tests first the one for the MRI won't be until tomorrow."

John replied back to his daughter, "Okay, I'm very happy that you are doing good."

John and Andrea arrived in Cleveland, Ohio. John sent a text to Sean at 5:05 p.m., "Just landed in Cleveland."

Sean responded, "I forgot to ask you if you knew how to use Uber."

John replied, "We have a rental car."

Sean texted back, "Ah ok," and John quickly added, "I am Uber!"

Sean replied, "I can only imagine you two using Uber now."

Sean thought it was probably best that his parents had rented a car while in Cleveland.

After picking up their luggage, John and Andrea headed to the rental car area. On their way through the airport, John could not help but notice a big display. It read, Welcome to Cleveland-Where the Legend Began... Superman "The World's Greatest Super Hero." Part of the display included a life-size statue of Superman along with interesting information about the creators of Superman, Jerry Siegel and Joe Shuster, who lived in Cleveland when they created Superman back in 1938. John stopped and took a picture of the display. He has been a lifelong fan of Superman. He smiled and told Andrea, "With Superman on Christie's side she is going to be okay."

Andrea smiled and said, "I sure hope so."

John and Andrea arrived at the Cleveland Clinic. What a big place! As they pulled up to the parking ramp across the street from the hospital, Andrea called Christie. "Hi, Mom!"

Andrea replied, "Hi, Honey, we are pulling into the parking ramp right now."

Christie said, "Great! How were your flights?"

Andrea said, "They were good. Your dad is glad to be off the planes."

Christie chuckled, "I'll have Brian meet you in the lobby. From what he has told me, this is a really big place."

Andrea said, "Okay, thanks. Yes, it is huge!"

The couple made their way via an underground tunnel to the lobby of the hospital. There they saw Brian waiting for them. They waved at him and he waved back. They gave Brian hugs and asked how he was doing. He said, "I'm doing all right. They haven't really told us what the next steps are and when Christie will have the surgery."

John said, "They are probably looking over all of her information in order to establish their plan of action. It wouldn't surprise me if they don't make her go through the same or more tests that she has already had. They are going to want to make sure they have a clear road map of what they are about to tackle."

Brian nodded and John continued, "That's a good thing." The three of them anxiously headed to Christie's room.

In Christie's room the foursome were once again reunited. Christie received hugs from her mom and dad. They were all glad to be back together. John asked Christie, "How was your flight?"

Christie smiled and said, "I had it pretty easy. They just wheeled my bed onto the plane, and I could stretch out and relax. Poor Brian had to sit on one of those little jump seats. So did the doctor and nurse."

Brian chimed in, "It wasn't too bad. It was a smooth flight and we got here pretty quick."

John said, "It's nice that they were able to send you that way. I can't imagine how uncomfortable it would have been for Christie on a commercial flight plus being exposed to lots of other people, and their germs, and having layovers."

Andrea chimed in, "Well, we are here now and these people here will help you get better."

Christie asked her parents if they were hungry. John said that he could go for something. Andrea didn't want to leave Christie and said she could wait a while. John asked where the cafeteria was, and Brian explained approximately where it was at and added that there were several other little restaurants next to the cafeteria to pick from. Brian also noted that he could not find a regular caffeinated soda on the entire place. All they sold was sugar-free or diet. John pointed out that they were in a heart hospital after all. John insisted that he was bringing something back for Andrea and she asked him to pick up a salad or some soup.

The two men made their way to the restaurant area. There were lots of people walking throughout. John mentioned that he had heard that people come from all over the world to get help at this hospital. John thought to himself that this building design as well as the building environment, reminded him of something out of a Star Trek movie. Brian said, "This is a city in a city."

Back in Texas, Christie's friend and coworker, Brandy Dastillon, had been busy. She wanted to help Christie and Brian as much as she could. She knew that they would have lots of medical expenses piling up, and she wanted to help. After the warm reception Christie gave Brandy Green for the T-shirt she made for Christie, Brandy Dastillon was inspired to design another in support for Christie that others could wear. This was an all-black T-shirt with red scripted lettering that read, The Beat Goes On, followed by the heart monitor wavelength with a heart shape in the middle, and just below that in red script, Christie's Journey. She posted a picture of the design on the Christie's Journey Facebook page along with the following: "We are taking preorders for shirts for the benefit of Christie Firth and her family. Shirts will be twenty dollars S–XL and twenty-five dollars for 2XL and larger. We are taking orders until June 28. Please PM me any orders you may have and we can make payment arrangements. All proceeds go to Christie & Brian Firth for any expenses they may incur at this time. Below is a copy of what it will look like. Thanks in advance!" Many friends and family responded and ordered T-shirts. One of the friends was Mike Wade. Police Officer Mike Wade. He posted, "Mike Wade, XL Please."

John's brother Joe responded, "Mike Wade, I will be taking care of the cost of your shirt, sir." John read his brother's response and was proud that Joe responded the way that he was going to, only Joe had beat him to it.

15

June 20, 2019

Andrea posted the following on Christie's Journey Facebook page, "No updates, no surgery set yet. Christie is doing good."

At 7:05 a.m. John received a text from Christie. It was a picture of her left arm. It looked swollen and bruised. The caption she typed with the picture read, "They are having to redo my IV."

John looked at the picture and felt terrible for his daughter. He replied back, "I'm sorry."

Christie told her dad, "It's okay."

John marveled at his daughter's courage and sent her a smiley face emoticon.

Christie had several visits that day by different members of the medical team. They were all excited to meet Christie. Their usual patients with this condition are children. Not many lived to adulthood with this condition. It has been a reminder for Christie and her family how blessed she has been.

There wasn't much for the family or Christie to do at this point in time. Christie was hooked to a heart monitor and there was someone from the hospital staff always keeping an eye on her monitor's output.

While sitting in Christie's room, Andrea accessed the internet search engine, Google and typed in "left coronary artery pathway." A drawing of the human heart appeared on her screen. It showed pictures of arteries of the heart with the names of the arteries next to the picture. The picture showed the right coronary artery, right marginal, left coronary artery, left marginal artery, and left anterior descending artery. Below the picture was the following information: "The two main *coronary arteries* are the *left* and right *coronary arteries*. The *left coronary artery* (LCA), which divides into the left anterior descending *artery* and the circumflex branch, supplies blood to the *heart* ventricles and *left* atrium."[6]

Andrea thought to herself, *My baby is going to have her heart operated on.* She held back her tears in order to have a strong front to help keep Christie's worries lessened.

John posted a picture of Brian and Christie sitting next to each other on the Christie's Journey Facebook page. Brian looked relaxed sitting next to his wife and Christie looked beautiful. She had her wonderful smile on her face. She was wearing her glasses, it was easier than dealing with her contacts, her hair was down and the patch for her heart monitor could be seen below her left clavicle as well as her hospital identification bracelet on her left wrist and also several bruises on her left arm from numerous blood draws and intravenous needle applications as well as a bandage from a recent blood draw. His caption read: "We are hanging out at the Cleveland Clinic in Cleveland, Ohio. Great people here and these two are ready to get things moving. All is well with Christie and she is ready to get her surgery over. Andy Bain and I are very thankful we are here!"

Christie's doctor and surgeon will be Dr. Hani Najm. Dr. Najm is a very nice man with a great bedside manner. He met with Christie and her family and was very confident that he and his team were going to fix Christie's problem with her heart. The visit made the nervous foursome feel much better.

Sometime later after the visit, one of the nurses stopped in to check Christie's vital signs and see if she needed anything else. She told Christie and her family that Dr. Najm is the best and that he had performed over five thousand of these surgeries. That information added to the family's confidence.

---

[6] Information courtesy of gwheartandvascular.org.

16

June 21, 2019

It's Brian and Christie's fifth wedding anniversary. Brian woke up. He was lying on the couch next to Christie's bed. Christie had been up for quite a while watching television with the volume turned low so it wouldn't wake up Brian. She smiled at her husband and said, "Happy anniversary, Love. I'm sorry we have to be here." Brian looked at his wife and said, "Happy anniversary. I'm sorry we have to be here too but I'm glad we are so we can get things right for you." They gave each other a hug and kiss.

Andrea and John made it back from their hotel. They brought Brian some breakfast from a local Burger King. He was glad to have some "not too healthy" food.

The weather in Cleveland this afternoon was beautiful. Christie's room had a large window and all spent lots of time looking out it and watching people below coming and going.

Christie's nurse came in and mentioned what a beautiful day it was outside. Andrea responded, "It sure looks like it." The nurse continued and said to Christie, "If you would like to go up on the roof and soak up a little sunshine and get some fresh air, you are welcomed to do so. You're monitor is remote so you can go up there and we can still keep a watch on you." Christie turned and asked Brian and her mom and dad, "Do you guys want to go up there?" They all nodded and said sure.

The four walked to the elevator and then made their way up to the rooftop observatory. They were all impressed. The elevator opened up to a big lobby-like room. There were big windows and the skyline of downtown Cleveland along with the beautiful Great Lake, Lake Erie were visible. They walked through some doors and onto the rooftop. The warm weather and sunshine felt good and very welcomed. They found a table to sit at and enjoy the change of atmosphere.

John smiled and said, "This is really nice up here. What a beautiful day!" John thought to himself how fortunate he was to be able to spend this time with his daughter, wife, and son-in-law. He thought to himself and reflected on how lucky he was. Then his thoughts went dark. What if this is one of the last times he gets to have with Christie? Tears welled up in his eyes. Christie asked, "What's wrong, Dad?"

John smiled and said, "I'm just happy we are all together. I love you, Honey."

Christie smiled and said, "Don't get upset. I love you too."

Andrea knows her husband well and said, "We now know what the problem is and now we can focus good thoughts on getting it fixed."

John knew Andrea was right. She is seldom ever wrong. John smiled at Andrea and said, "You are absolutely right, dear!"

Christie tired and Brian commandeered a wheelchair for his wife for a ride back down to her room.

17

June 22–23, 2019

The days are long when you are in this situation. Christie kept getting different tests done on her heart and was monitored twenty-four hours a day. She was visited by different teams of medical personnel. All were learning about Christie's condition and also assessing different ideas and approaches on how to proceed with her treatment. Christie and Andrea were very frustrated.

"It's time to get moving on this surgery and fix her heart!" Andrea said this right after a group of medical personnel had just left Christie's room.

Christie responded, "Why don't they get moving with this?"

John wanted to be reassuring but he also knew he had to be blunt with these two headstrong women. John said, "You knew when we came here that they would want to run through more tests and even the same tests that have already been done in Texarkana. They aren't going to go into surgery not armed with the most information and the best plan to make things better. They are going to go at their own pace. We are in their system and we need to be patient so they can do the best job for you. I know it's hardest for you, Christie, all this waiting. We just need to wait and be as helpful and patient, and the next thing you know they will be ready for your surgery."

Christie looked at her dad and said, "I know, I just want to get through this and get back home to my babies."

John looked at his daughter and smiled. "We all want the same thing, Honey."

The foursome passed their time with more trips to the roof-top for fresh air and sunshine. They also played many games of the dice games Farkle and Yahtzee and had lots of smiles and laughs. Of course there were times when they cried too.

Christie also got lots of calls and texts from family and friends in both Texas, Iowa, and Illinois. She has lots of people pulling for her. This included daily phone calls and pictures of Westin via text from her best friend, Ms. Paula. Paula is an angel living on this Earth. She has been a godsend for Christie and her family. All wanted Westin to be with them but all also knew that Paula was taking good care and loving him. It made things easier.

Natalie called Christie from Texas to see how her mom was doing. "Hi, Momma, when are you coming home?"

Christie smiled and put on a brave front for her daughter. "Hi, Baby, I'm going to have surgery in a couple of days and then I will be able to come home shortly after that." This was a lot for a seven-year-old to comprehend. They talked a little more and Natalie seemed to be satisfied with Christie's answers. Brian also spoke to his daughter and asked her if she was being a good girl and to help out as much as she could. The couple told Natalie they loved her and both hoped what they told her was true.

Another Sunday arrived. Pastor Dave Schooley of the Eicher Emmanuel Mennonite Church updated the congregation of Christie's status. He shared that their prayers and good thoughts were still needed. Lora Bain and the congregation prayed for Christie and her family.

18

June 24, 2019

The weekend was nice but everyone was starting to become anxious in anticipation of Christie's upcoming surgery. Time dragged slowly on this Monday. The foursome did their best to pass the time. All would get lost in their own thoughts from moment to moment, praying that everything would go well during the surgery and that this would help return Christie to good health.

Then, finally, Christie and her family received the news that they had been hoping and praying for. She would have the surgery tomorrow. All were excited and all were nervous. What they have been wanting was now almost here. It was scheduled. What happens after?

Christie received a phone call from her good friend, April Thompson. "Hi, Sweetie, how are you doing?"

Christie was glad to speak with her friend. "Things are going to start happening," Christie told her friend.

April responded, "Have they scheduled your surgery?"

Christie said, "Yes, it's going to happen sometime tomorrow afternoon."

April said, "Oh my! That's coming up quick. James and I want to be there for you. We will get a flight and be there."

Christie told her friend, "You don't have to come all the way here."

April cut in, "We want to. I'm going to hang up and get our airline tickets right now. I love you and I will see you tomorrow!"

Christie hung up her phone and said, "April and James are coming. They want to be here when I'm having my surgery." The three smiled at Christie.

Andrea posted on Christie's Journey Facebook page: "Tomorrow is the big surgery, sometime in the afternoon. Suppose to be a 6 hour surgery, with three surgeons. More info to follow. Prayers to the surgeons and Christie!" John also posted on Christie's Journey Facebook page, he included a selfie photo of Christie in her bed, Brian in a chair next to her, Andrea at the foot of her bed, and John holding the camera in front of the three. His post read: "Christie Firth's surgery is tomorrow. She is ready, we are ready and the Medical Team is ready. Please continue to pray for all of us, especially Christie and the Medical Team. Thanks to everyone for your support. Our family is overwhelmed with your kindness!"

Andrea contacted Sean in Iowa and told him about the surgery now being scheduled. Sean told his mother he was on his way and would be there tomorrow. It would be an eight-and-a-half-hour drive for Sean. Andrea told Sean to be careful and that she loved him and would see him tomorrow.

19

June 25, 2019

It's exactly two weeks to the day that Christie experienced cardiac arrest in Hooks, Texas. Now she will continue her fight in the hands of Dr. Hani Najm and his surgical team, 1,020 miles from Hooks, Texas, in Cleveland, Ohio. The doctor and his staff know what the problem is and they have, what they determined to be, a successful plan to initiate and execute.

April and James Thompson arrived in time from Texas, to wish Christie all the best during her surgery. Christie and Brian were glad to see their friends and have them there. Sean was driving toward Cleveland and wished Christie good luck over the telephone.

At 10:30 a.m. a couple of nurses arrived in Christie's room. The female nurse said, "Good morning! We are here to take you over to the pediatric wing of the hospital so you can have your surgery. Dr. Najm and his team are ready for you."

Christie smiled nervously and said, "Okay, I'm ready. Can they go with me?" She referenced Brian, Andrea, John, April, and James.

"Yes, you can all come along. Of course you will have to wait in the waiting room. It's a Ronald McDonald House waiting room. It's nice and you will be comfortable in there." Then the nurse smiled and said, "I have to zap your identification bracelet to make sure we have the right patient going to the right place." Christie lifted her left arm and the nurse *zapped* her identification bracelet. She had the right patient.

The group walked with Christie as she was pushed by the nurses to the pediatric side of the hospital. They got on an elevator and went down to the lowest level of the hospital. They went through a labyrinth of hallways and then to another elevator. It was quite a distance. They all got on the elevator and made their way toward the operating room. The nurses stopped in front of a set of double doors.

The female nurse said to Christie, "Well, Christie, we are here. You want to tell everyone that you will see them after your surgery?" Christie's support team put on their best faces.

April and James hugged Christie and wished her good luck.

Andrea hugged her daughter and told her, "You've got this. You're going to be much better after the surgery and I'll see you then."

Christie looked at her mom and said, "I love you, Mom."

Andrea smiled and said, "I love you too, Peanut."

John approached Christie and said, "You be strong in there and we'll be strong out here for you." He barely got the words out. He was trying not to cry. He knew he needed to be strong for his daughter.

Christie said to John, "I will be, Dad, and I'm going to be okay. I love you."

John smiled and said, "I love you too." He kissed Christie on her cheek.

Brian went to his wife. He said, "I love you, Babe. Everything is going to be okay. I'll be waiting for you."

Christie smiled and hugged and kissed Brian. She told him, "Thanks, Babe, I love you too." Another nurse approached the group and offered to escort them to the waiting room. The nurses pushed Christie through the double doors.

The group made it to the Ronald McDonald House waiting room. A lady named Georgia introduced herself. She is a volunteer. She let everyone know they were welcome to help themselves to snacks and drinks. There were a couple of round tables with chairs that people could pass the time at playing board games or just visiting. There were also two big couches and a couple of reclining chairs in the room, along with a tabletop version *old school* Galaga and Asteroids video game. There were several other people waiting for their loved ones to come out of surgery too. Over time, John and

Andrea would learn that Christie was the oldest patient in surgery. The other relatives of the other patients were waiting on their loved ones, that were in their late teenage years down to an infant. This information really underscored to John, Andrea, and Brian on how rare Christie's situation is.

In the operating room the nurse put warm blankets on Christie. "How does that feel, Christie?"

Christie said, "That feels really good."

The nurse smiled and said, "Good. We want you to be comfortable. Would you like to listen to some music?"

Christie said, "Sure."

The nurse said, "What kind of music do you like?"

Christie responded, "It doesn't matter."

The nurse selected a song but Christie didn't hear it. She was out. The anesthesia had done its job.

At 11:23 a.m. John sent a text to his brother Joe, "She is now in the surgery room. Four to six hours to go."

Joe replied, "She's at the best place for this still praying."

John replied to his brother, "Yes she is, thanks."

Andrea was texting to her friends and family. She and April were having a nice visit and Brian was being entertained by James. John was glad that Brian had a distraction.

John realized that an update should be posted on the Christie's Journey Facebook page, so he did. It read: "Okay, everyone, Christie is now in the surgery room. The process will take anywhere from 4-6 hours. Thanks for all of your good thoughts and prayers from all of us!"

Georgia reminded the group that there was food and drink available, but no one was ready for that at this time.

Shortly after 1:00 p.m., a nurse stopped into the waiting room and let the group know that things were starting to happen and an incision had been made. John wondered why it took an hour and a half before the incision was made and then quickly reminded himself, he didn't have a medical degree.

At 3:15 p.m., the anxious group received another update. The doctor is currently in the process of moving the artery to the proper side of her heart. She is doing well and expect another update in an hour or so.

About fifteen minutes later, Dr. Najm appeared in the waiting room. He had a happy look on his face and that instantly relieved everyone's nerves. He asked, "Are you all Christie's family?"

The group replied in unison, "Yes!"

The doctor turned toward Brian, "You are Christie's husband, correct?"

Brian replied, "Yes, sir."

Dr. Najm shook Brian's hand. He then went on, "All went very well. She should feel a lot better now. I have done lots of these surgeries before on children, not so many on adults. Things went very well and she is being sewn up right now."

Brian thanked the doctor as did Andrea, John, April, and James.

John posted the following on the Christie's Journey Facebook page: "Christie's Doctor just met with us. Her surgery went very well! She did very good through it. They are sewing her up as I type. Thank you all for your good thoughts and prayers. Please keep praying for her. Our God is good!" The post received 119 likes and loves and thirty-six comments of well-wishing and congratulations along with continued prayers.

Sean arrived from Iowa shortly after. Everyone was glad to see him, and he was relieved that his sister's surgery went so well. John challenged his son to a couple of games of Asteroids. Sean was glad to oblige.

At 10:20 p.m. John received a text from Joe. "How's Christie and you guys doing?"

John replied to his brother, "She is doing well. They don't make enough sedation to keep her down. She heard our voices and tries to communicate with us. If all keeps on the right track, she will get out of intensive care unit on Thursday morning. Andrea's nerves are catching up with her but on a whole if things keep on the right track, we will all be okay. Sean is here. He got here before Christie was put in ICU so he has gotten to say hello to her too. We are back at the hotel room now and calling it a day."

Joe replied back, "Get some rest."

John typed back to his brother, "That's the plan."

20

John sent the following text to his sister, Joni: "She is having several tubes removed from her right now including tubes in her chest and neck. Has a slight sore throat from when she had the breathing tube in. Otherwise doing quite well. She is amazing!"

Joni responded, "Yay, that's great news!" It was 10:21 a.m.

John received a text from his best friend Donnie Jones. Donnie lives in LeClaire, Iowa, and he was checking in on his friend and seeing how Christie was doing: "How is everyone doing today?"

John responded to his friend letting him know Christie's current condition. John texted Donnie, "She is amazing!"

Donnie texted back, "Absolutely, she is Bainstrong!"

John smiled at his friend's comment and sent him back an emoticon of an arm flexing.

Christie was recovering in the pediatric intensive care unit. She was the oldest patient on the floor. There were several children who had different heart ailments that were also recovering from surgeries. She wasn't feeling the best right now. It was a long surgery and she was experiencing discomfort and nausea.

Sean knew the best thing for his sister at this time was to get lots of rest. Sean is a huge Major League Baseball fan and the team that he follows the closest is the St. Louis Cardinals. While checking what was going on in the league via his smartphone, he happened to see that the Indians were at home today at Progressive Field and they were hosting the Kansas City Royals. Sean asked his dad what he thought if he were to attend the game that afternoon. John responded, "I think that is a great idea. Go over there and try to enjoy yourself. I would go with you under different circumstances but I need to stay here with your sister. This will be a good game to go to. You won't care who wins or loses." Sean thanked his dad. He loves his sister but he needed to get away for just a little while and he was ready for the distraction.

Sean made his way to the elevator. When the elevator doors opened up there were three ladies with three service dogs. He let them exit and then entered the elevator. He quickly sent a text to Andrea, "Some women with service dogs just got off the elevator. It looks like they are headed to the ICU." Andrea saw the text but didn't say anything to the others. She responded to Sean, "Neat. Try to enjoy the game."

Andrea, Brian, and John were visiting Christie when she got a knock on her door. There were two young ladies standing at the doorway. Each had a beautiful dog on a leash. They asked if they could come in and say hi. The group said of course. One of the dogs was a standard poodle. Its name was Tortilla. The other dog was a nice golden retriever with the name Charity. Both dogs took turns coming to Christie's bedside. They enjoyed her petting them. Christie was feeling nauseous and quickly turned to her dad and quietly said, "Get them out of here I'm going to throw up." John quickly made sure that Christie had something to throw up in, close by her as he simultaneously thanked the ladies and their dogs for stopping in while apologizing for having to wrap up the visit so quickly. Both young ladies figured out quickly what was happening and made their way out of the room. Christie vomited and felt bad for what had just happened. Everyone assured her not to worry about it.

Christie needed rest. Brian and John went out to the waiting room while Andrea stayed with her daughter. It was hard for everyone to see Christie this way. They could only imagine what she was going through.

Christie's friend, Jessi Sisemore, shared the following post on the Christie's Journey Facebook page: "Here are what the bracelets look like that I've made. They should be in by July 3. They're $5 each and the funds will go to Christie and her family to pay medical bills and help cover expenses while she's been off work. If you'd like one please let me know. I can ship them as well as long as you cover shipping fees. Thanks so much." The post also had a picture of what the bracelet looks like. It has a red-and-black background with the words "Christie's Journey" in white lettering along with the heart beat monitor symbol with a heart in the middle.

Christie and her family were so thankful for Jessi's efforts and thoughtfulness.

A little later, April and James stopped by to see Christie before they headed back to Texas. They were happy her surgery went so well and that she was feeling better today. They wished her the best and looked forward to seeing her back home. Christie and Brian thanked and hugged their friends. It was so nice of them to come all the way to Cleveland to be with them during this time.

21

June 27, 2019

Andrea posted on the Christie's Journey Facebook page: "Yesterday was a rough one, she was sick all day. Praying for a better day."

After breakfast, a nurse came in to escort Christie on the first of many walks that she would be taking today. Brian asked if he could go along and the nurse said of course.

The nurse was guarded as she helped Christie to sit up on the side of the bed. She really had not been up but to use the bathroom and the nurse wanted to make sure Christie wasn't light-headed when she stood up. The nurse said, "How do you feel?"

Christie smiled and said, "Pretty good."

The nurse then asked, "Do you want to try to stand up now?"

Brian was standing next to the bed as well and was ready to help his wife the best that he could.

Christie said, "Yes, let's give it a try."

The nurse smiled, "Okay, give me your hands, and I will hold mine in place while you use them to pull yourself up."

Christie followed the instructions and quickly had her bearings.

The nurse said, "Are you ready?"

Christie said, "Yes, I am." Christie made her way out of the room with the nurse on one side and Brian on the other. John and Andrea stayed in the room and watched with pride as their daughter started out the door. Sean turned to his parents and said, "She is doing really well." John and Andrea nodded at their son.

Christie was rapidly improving from her status of the day before. She was doing well enough to be moved out of the ICU to a regular room to continue her recovery. Her EF rate was currently at 45–50% and Dr. Najm was anticipating more improvement. Her family was very thankful.

Tomorrow would be Friday. As of tomorrow, it will be thirteen working days since the last time John had been at work. With Christie doing so well, and Christie's release coming very soon, he and Andrea decided it would be best for him to head back home and get back to work on Monday. Sean needed to go back to Iowa as well. John would leave with Sean in the morning to head home. He didn't like leaving but knew it was for the best. He was grateful to have Sean to do the upcoming driving.

22

Andrea posted the following to the Christie's Journey Facebook page: "Christie is doing so much better since being moved out of the pediatrics ICU, yesterday afternoon. She will be going for numerous walks today. Thanks for everyone's Prayers and Support. Doctors are great here."

Back in Texas, Kelly McCullough posted a picture on the Christie's Journey Facebook page along with the following caption: "Christie's Journey shirt makers working hard!" The picture was of Brandy Dastillon, Paula Burns, and Kelly; holding up the decals in preparation of applying them to the T-shirts. Christie was overwhelmed by her friends' generosity.

Later in the day, Nurse Practitioner Adolpho, stopped in to check Christie's vitals and to see if she needed anything.

He asked, "How are you feeling, Christie?"

Christie responded, "I'm feeling okay. Have you heard when I can go home?"

Adolpho smiled and responded, "I have not heard a 'for certain' day but I can tell you I think it will be very soon. Let's concentrate on taking your walks and doing your breathing treatments and keeping you comfortable and before you know it, it will be time to go."

Christie smiled and said, "Okay, I'll do that. But if you hear anything will you let me know?"

Adolpho replied, "I sure will. Now it is time for your breathing treatment. Let me see how you can do."

Christie looked over at her mom. She knew that if her dad were here right now, he would be smiling because he had made it his responsibility to make sure Christie was keeping up with the breathing treatments. He didn't want his daughter to catch pneumonia. Christie breathed in and out of the spirometer and Adolpho was very impressed at how well she did.

Later on Christie had another echocardiogram. The results came back with very good news. Her EF was still in the 45–50% range. Brian was outside of Christie's room discussing the results and options with Adolpho. Adolpho told Brian, "She is doing very well. The next thing is to install the defibrillator. The tricky part is, scheduling. It is very hard to get things scheduled here. There are a lot of patients waiting in line. If we schedule the procedure today, it may be next Friday before it is actually done."

Brian looked at Adolpho with a dejected look on his face. Brian said, "She wants to get back home so badly. We've been gone for a long time. Is there any way she can do this back home?"

Adolpho smiled and said, "Let me discuss with Dr. Najm. With as well as her EF is, there is a good possibility that she could go back home and have the procedure done in Texas."

Brian smiled. "I just want to do the best for Christie. Thank you, sir."

The two men shook hands and Brian went back into the room.

Andrea was concerned about the hotel bills that had been mounting up as well as other bills. Andrea was very blessed that her good friend Jennifer Vernon, back in Iowa, who Christie calls "Aunt Jen Bunny" insisted on helping with some of the lodging bills and called the hotel that John, Andrea, and Sean had been staying at and she paid for part of their stay there over the phone. Andrea has been a longtime fan of the Ronald McDonald House and what they do to help families of ill patients and decided she would try to see if she could spend the next couple of nights there. Fortunately there was a Ronald McDonald House just a few blocks from the hospital. They had room for Andrea and she spent this night there. Andrea and her family were very grateful for the hospitality and the fact that it cost around sixty dollars to stay the night.

23

June 29, 2019

Today is Brian's thirty-third birthday. This young man has been through a gauntlet of emotions and events the past eighteen days; he almost lost his wife, he celebrated his first Father's Day with Westin, his wedding anniversary, and the medical plane flight to Cleveland, his wife's heart surgery and now her recovery from that surgery. Christie and Andrea did their best to make Brian's day special. He told them his best gift was to have Christie on the road to recovery. Christie and Andrea smiled at Brian.

Andrea left the couple for a while so they could have some privacy. Christie said to Brian, "I'm so sorry we have to be here on your birthday, Babe."

Brian looked at Christie and held her hands, "Don't ever be sorry for this. It is nothing you had any control over. I'm so glad you are still here with me and that you are going to get better. I love you so much, Christie."

Christie smiled at the love of her life and said, "I love you too."

Brian looked at his wrist and the new watch he was wearing and said to Christie, "When did you have time to get this for me?"

Christie smiled and said, "I ordered it while I was in the hospital in Texarkana. April brought it here for me so I could give it to you today."

Brian looked at his wife and said, "You didn't have to do that."

Christie smiled and replied, "I wanted to."

That afternoon Christie and Brian received a surprise they were waiting for. It had been determined earlier in the day that Christie will need a defibrillator and that she can have it installed by Dr. Hayes back in Texarkana. Adolpho and another nurse came in with a LifeVest. They were there to get Christie fitted to wear this device as comfortable as possible while also allowing the device to be at its maximum efficiency.

The LifeVest wearable cardioverter defibrillator (WCD) is worn by patients at risk of sudden cardiac death (SCD). The heart's electrical system controls the heartbeat. When this system fails, it may trigger a dangerously fast heartbeat. This fast heartbeat causes the heart to quiver or shake instead of pumping blood to the body and brain. When this happens, you can suddenly pass out. This is sudden cardiac arrest (SCA). It occurs without warning. Without treatment, death occurs in minutes. This is sudden cardiac death (SCD).

A defibrillator is a device that is used to control dangerously fast heart rhythms by applying an electrical shock to the heart. While some defibrillator devices are implanted under the skin, the LifeVest WCD is worn directly against the patient's skin. When worn as directed, the device can provide a constant safeguard against SCD. The WCD is designed to detect a life-threatening rapid heart rhythm and automatically deliver a treatment shock to save the wearer's life. No matter where the person is or the time of day, the LifeVest WCD can provide sudden cardiac death protection. It can protect the wearer even when they are alone. It is therefore critical that the person in need wear the LifeVest WCD at all times-including while they sleep.[7] After being explained all of this, Christie and Brian understood very well the importance of a proper fitting. Christie would be wearing this until a permanent defibrillator is installed under her skin.

Christie was concerned and scared and hid those emotions the best that she could. She wanted out of the hospital and to get back to her life in Texas. She knew she had more hoops to jump through and would continue to do so. She stayed focused on the end goal of having her life back.

---

[7]   Information courtesy of lifevest.zoll.com.

Brian called Andrea. "Hi, Brian, what have you heard?"

Brian answered his mother-in-law, "They got Christie fitted for a LifeVest. It's a vest that has a defibrillator in it that she will need to wear until the permanent defibrillator is installed under her skin. She said it is kind of uncomfortable but they are getting it to fit her the best that it can."

Andrea responded, "Wow! Does that mean she can go home tomorrow?"

Brian said, "Yes, ma'am, I believe so."

Andrea processed the information and quickly responded, "Then I will check on flights for us. Tell Christie I will take care of all the details."

Brian was glad that Andrea was still there in Cleveland with them. He answered back, "Thank you. We will see you in a little bit."

Andrea called John to give him an update. "Christie has been fitted with a LifeVest, that's a vest that has a defibrillator built into it and it monitors her heart. She will have to wear it for the next sixty days but she gets to go home tomorrow!" John listened to his wife and as he listened, tears welled up in his eyes.

He said to Andrea, "She really gets to go home tomorrow?"

Andrea responded, "Yes, she really does."

John said, "Oh, that is so wonderful. Should I bring your Jeep out there so we can all ride together back to Texas?"

Andrea quickly responded, "No, Honey, we are going to fly back to Texas."

John quickly asked, "Is flying on a commercial airline where you will be packed in like sardines the best for Christie? I could leave now and be there in time for her release in the morning and then you or Brian could drive for a while until I rested up."

Like John, Andrea wanted the best for their daughter and having him drive from Iowa to Ohio and then to Texas wasn't the best idea for any of them. She told John, "If the doctors here didn't think she should go on a commercial flight then they would have said so. They have okayed this and it will be a shorter time for Christie to experience discomfort. If we were in the car it would take forever." John thought to himself that once again, Andrea, the voice of reason, had it under control. John told his wife, "Okay, but I need to have updates throughout this trip back." Andrea smiled and told her husband that she would keep him informed.

Andrea returned to the hospital. Christie had asked Andrea earlier if she would take Brian out for a birthday dinner. Andrea asked Brian if he would like to go out for dinner.

Brian replied, "If it's okay with you could we pick something up and come back here and eat it? That way Christie can have some too."

Andrea smiled. "Of course we can." Andrea then ordered Chinese food and Brian accompanied her on the Uber ride to get it. Once back, they shared with Christie and all were thankful they would be heading to Texas in the morning.

24

June 30, 2019

Twenty days since Christie had last been at her home. Today she was going home. She would be back in Simms, Texas, for the first time since she left for work the morning of June 11th.

Christie was excited, joyous, nervous, worried, concerned, and grateful all at the same time. She was going home! She was going to be with her kids again in her house. Although she would be wearing a LifeVest until a permanent defibrillator was installed under her skin, the most important thing was reuniting with her family.

She didn't sleep much throughout the night in anticipation of her trip home. As far as Christie was concerned 9:00 a.m. couldn't come soon enough. That's the time her mom had arranged for the taxi to arrive to take them to the airport.

At 7:00 a.m. Andrea arrived in Christie's room and smiled at her and Brian. "Good morning! Are you two ready to get out of here?"

Christie smiled and Brian answered for both of them, "Yes, ma'am!"

Andrea reminded them that the cardiac limo would be ready to transport them to the airport for their flight to Dallas at nine.

Christie had breakfast and prepared for her journey back to Texas. This is the first time she had worn her own clothes since June 11th. Brian had packed clothes for her before they left Texas so she would be ready to go as soon as they got the okay. Even though she was wearing the LifeVest underneath her top, it felt very good and normal to be in her own clothing.

Around 8:30 a.m., a nurse came into Christie's room with a piece of paper. She said, "Good morning! I hear someone is going to go home today. How exciting! I have a prescription here that you will need to get filled before you go."

Andrea reached out and took the prescription. Andrea told the nurse, "We are scheduled to leave here at nine, where do I go to get this filled?"

The nurse responded that the pharmacy was in the building across the street from the hospital. Andrea told everyone that she would hurry over there and get the prescription filled.

Andrea arrived at the pharmacy. It was closed. The sign on the door said that it would be open at eleven. Andrea was frustrated. No way were they going to miss their plane. Her daughter was going home today!

Andrea hurried back to Christie's floor and went straight to the nurses' station. She looked at the nurses gathered there and said, "I'm Andrea Bain, Christie Firth's mother."

The nurses listened to Andrea and one of them said, "Of course, Mrs. Bain, what can I do for you?"

Andrea responded in a matter-of-fact tone, "My daughter is scheduled to leave here at 9:00 a.m. so that we can get on a plane to Dallas. She needs this prescription filled before we leave, and I went across the street to the pharmacy to get this filled and it doesn't open until eleven." The nurse could tell that Andrea was disturbed and offered to check into it for her quickly. Andrea thanked her and headed to Christie's room.

Shortly after arriving in Christie's room the nurse appeared with enough of the prescription to get the trio back to Texas. All were grateful and all thanked the nurse for her extra efforts.

It was time to go. A nurse showed up with a wheelchair and Brian and Andrea grabbed the luggage. It's been quite an experience and the three were so grateful for the caring professionals here that helped Christie. Once outside on the ground floor, Christie breathed in the fresh air. Aside from the visits to the rooftop, she had not really been outside at all. The cardiac group provided transportation to the airport for their patients. When Andrea first heard that they were being provided with a limo, she assumed some sort of van or SUV. This was a very nice car, a Chrysler 300! Andrea, Brian, and Christie were quite impressed and loaded up into the car. They were on their way to Texas!

Andrea posted the following to the Christie's Journey Facebook Page along with a picture of Christie standing next to Adolpho: "Update Update!!! We r headed home. Thanks to all the doctors and staff! Nurse Practitioner Adolpho is one of our favorites. Cleveland Clinic. She is wearing a life vest for the next 60 days to determine if a defibrillator is needed. Let us get home and settled for a few days. Thank you for all of your love and support!" The post received 132 likes and loves and sixty-one comments of congratulations, well wishes, and prayers.

Later that morning at the Eicher Emmanuel Mennonite Church in Wayland, Iowa, Pastor Dave Schooley had come to the moment of his service where he asks the congregation if they have any prayer requests. Today it was teenager, Danny Baldosier's turn to walk throughout the sanctuary with a microphone so that the members of the congregation that had requests could be heard. Lora Bain raised her hand and waited for Danny to approach. Danny aimed the microphone in front of Lora. Lora smiled and said, "I just received an update before church this morning that my great niece Christie has been released from the Cleveland Clinic hospital and she is flying home. She should be in the air as I speak." Looks of happy faces, encouragement, and quiet praises to the Lord came from the congregation. Lora smiled and said, "Thank you."

The traveling trio landed in Dallas, Texas, around 1:00 p.m. Christie was rather uncomfortable with the LifeVest but didn't focus on that. She was focused on reuniting with Natalie and Westin and just being home soon.

Andrea texted April Thompson, "Hey, Doll, we should be home in an hour or two. Christie is worn out from plane ride and drive. She didn't sleep well last night. I bet she will tonight."

April quickly replied back, "Oh wow! Y'all are flying today! Lol I bet she does too!! So happy she's coming home!!" April ended her text with a smiley face emoticon.

Andrea rented a car at the Dallas Airport and the three headed to Simms, Texas. They arrived at the Firth home around 5:00 p.m.

Christie had contacted Paula while still in Dallas. She was ready to see Westin! Paula was so excited that her friend was coming home and assured her she would bring Westin home right away. Natalie was with her biological mother and would be reunited with Christie, Brian, and Westin very soon.

Andrea headed back to the Texarkana Airport to drop off the rental car and to pick up her and John's car that had been there since they flew to Cleveland. Christie was very tired and in a lot of pain. She knew that there was no way she could have rode home in a car all the way from Cleveland. The plane trip today and the two and a half hour car trip from Dallas was excruciating. Christie was questioning herself if it was truly a good idea to come home today or should she have stayed at the Cleveland Clinic a while longer? The pain from her surgery was immense.

About twenty minutes after arriving home, Paula arrived with Westin and her children, Caleb and Abbi. They were so excited to have Christie home!

Brian met Paula and the kids at the front door. It was a symphony of joyful noise! Brian hugged Paula and took Westin, who was strapped in his car seat, and invited Caleb and Abbi in. Paula went straight to Christie who was trying to relax on her couch recliner. She could tell her friend was in pain. Paula said, "How are you doing, Sweetie? You look like you aren't feeling good." They gently hugged.

Christie responded, "I'm very sore from where I had the surgery and this LifeVest I have to wear is kind of tight. It's so good to be home and to see you. Thank you for taking care of my kids. I don't know what we would have done without you, Paula."

Paula teared up a little and said, "I'm just so happy you are home! Westin was a perfect baby. Natalie played well with Abbi and Caleb. Just because you are home doesn't mean I won't be around to help you. If you need anything Christie, I will be there for you."

Christie told her friend, "I know. I love you, girl." The two friends smiled at each other.

Brian walked over to Christie while holding little Westin. Christie smiled and put her arms out, "How's my little man?" Brian gently placed Westin on Christie's lap and continued to hold Westin's weight while Christie loved on him. Westin instantly relaxed and recognized his momma. He was content. At that moment Christie was no longer thinking she might have left Cleveland too soon.

Brian, Christie, Natalie & Westin Firth

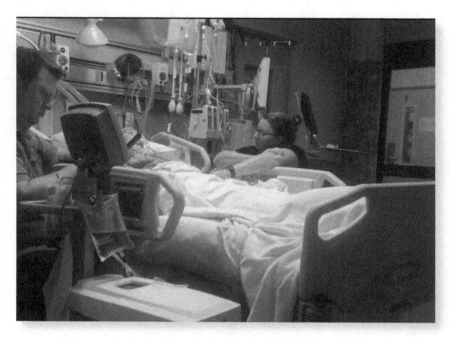

John sits bedside along with Christie's friend April, during
the cooling down process of Christie's body temperature
at Christus St. Michael Hospital in Texarkana, Texas.

Christie shows off her new t-shirt.

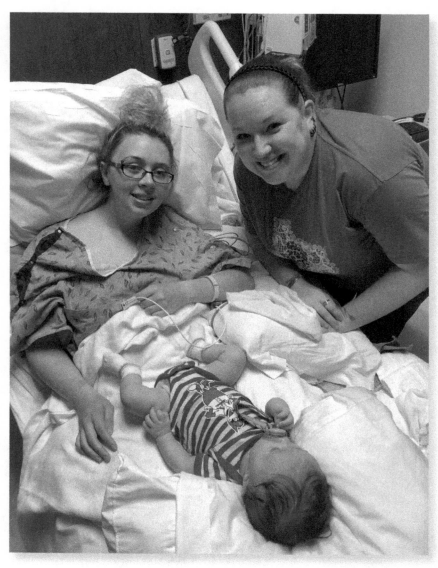

Paula brings Westin to visit his momma at
Christus St. Michael in Texarkana, Texas.

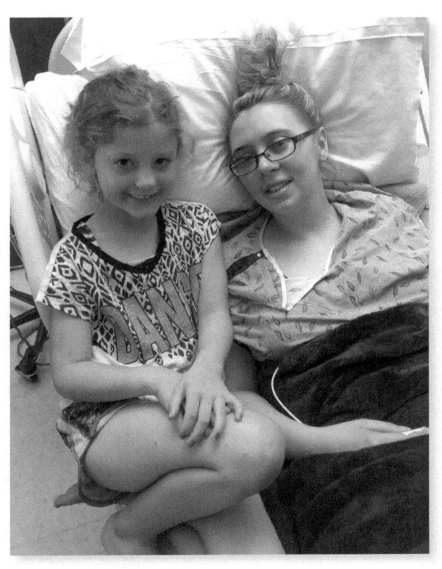

Natalie is happy to be with her momma at Christus
St. Michael Hospital in Texarkana, Texas.

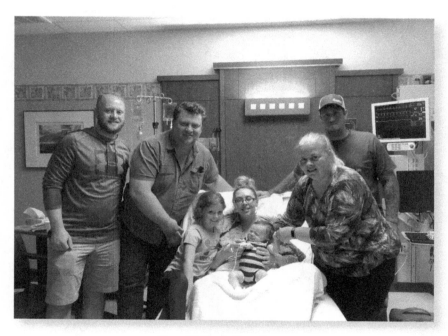

Best Father's Day Ever!

COL York presents Officer Wade a Commander's
Coin for his heroic and life-saving actions.

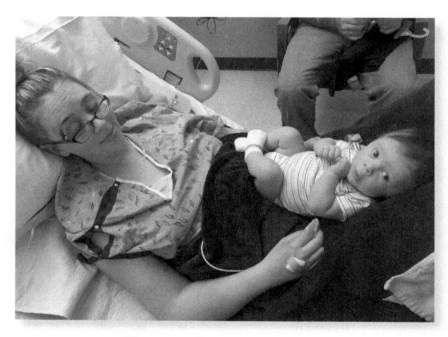

Westin visits his momma before she
leaves for Cleveland, Ohio.

The medical transport plane standing by in
Texarkana to take Christie to Cleveland, Ohio.

Welcome to Cleveland—Where the Legend
Began, Cleveland Airport, Cleveland, Ohio.

All is well with Christie and she is ready for her surgery.

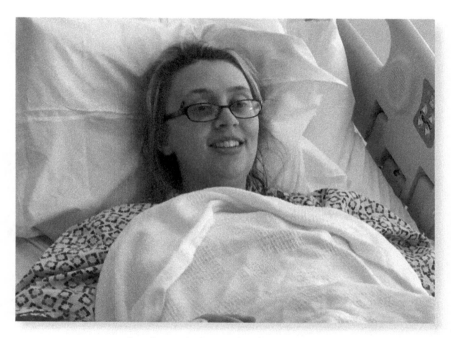

Our brave lady at Cleveland Clinic.

Enjoying sunshine and fresh air on the
rooftop of Cleveland Clinic.

Christie and Brian on the rooftop of the Cleveland
Clinic with the Cleveland skyline in the background.

Selfie photo the night before Christie's heart
surgery at the Cleveland Clinic.

Christie gets a visit in the ICU after her
surgery from Tortilla the service dog.

Service dog, Charity, brings a smile to
Christie after her surgery.

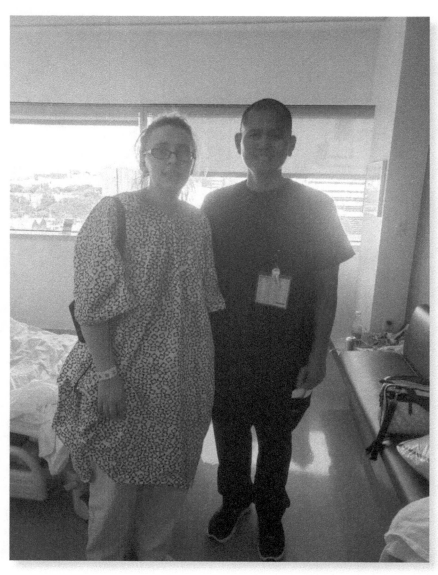

Nurse Practitioner Adolpho wishes Christie all the best on her last day at the Cleveland Clinic.

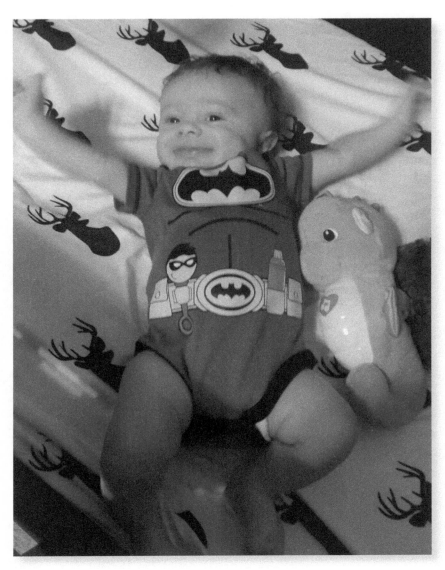

It's good to be home!

Christie gets a little wind therapy on Dad's new lawnmower.

25

July 3, 2019

Several days of rest is what the doctor ordered, and Andrea was making sure Christie was getting just that. Andrea was in full "Gigi" mode making sure that Westin was being cared for and that Christie was able to rest and Brian was able to head back to work knowing that his wife and child were being well looked after.

Christie's friend, Jessi Sisemore, posted on Christie's Journey's Facebook page: "The bracelets are here! Get one while they last. $5 each and all proceeds go to Christie Firth and Brian Firth to help cover costs while she's been off work due to medical conditions. Thank you all for your support!!! I have toddler, youth, and adult sizes available." She included a picture of many of the bracelets. Lots of people responded that they wanted one and Sean Bain asked if the post could be made public so he could share on his own personal page. Jessi responded to Sean that she would love to if he showed her how. Sean obliged.

Today was extra special. Natalie was being reunited with her family! Andrea picked Natalie up at her grandparents' house and brought Natalie home to be with everyone. This is the first time they were all together since Christie and Brian's flight to Cleveland.

Andrea opened the door to the house. "Hello, is anyone home?" Natalie was standing closely behind Andrea. She was anxious and concerned. She didn't know what to expect when she saw Christie again for the first time since she was in the hospital. Christie was sitting on her couch recliner. She said, "Who is at the door? Gigi, is someone behind you?" Natalie poked her head around Andrea and said, "Hello." She had a big smile on her face that matched both Christie's and Brian's. Christie continued to smile and said to Natalie, "Hey there, girl, don't be shy with me. Get over here!" Natalie skipped over to Christie and gave her a hug. She noticed something wasn't quite right and felt around Christie's ribs, touching the LifeVest. Natalie said, "What is under there, Momma?"

Christie replied, "Oh, that's a vest I have to wear under my shirt that helps me stay safe in case my heart doesn't want to work right."

Natalie looked at Christie and then touched around where the vest was and said, "Does it hurt you?"

Christie motioned her head no and said, "No, Honey, it's there to help me. It does make me a little sore though but I'm okay." That seemed to satisfy the seven-year-old's curiosity.

26

July 5, 2019

Paula Simmons was alone in her car. The kids were with Daniel and she was ready to get after her errands. Paula looked at her Christie's Journey bracelet and decided to make a video for her friend Christie. She grabbed her phone and from the driver's seat of her car, she proceeded to record her message. "Okay, hi, Christie!" Paula waved to the camera, flipped up her sunglasses over her forehead, and continued, "I just wanted to do this for you, okay? You know the story behind this bracelet, but this has been tattooed on me so it's not going anywhere." She removed the bracelet, stretched it out in front of the camera, and set it down. "After thirteen years, I'm takin' it off today." Then she held up the Christie's Journey bracelet in front of the camera and said, "Because you, my other best friend, are going on here." She then placed the Christie's Journey bracelet on her right wrist. She made sure it fit well and then said, "We love you, see you tonight!" Paula posted her video to Christie on the Christie's Journey Facebook page. Christie left a comment with the video, "Love you too, girl!" Andrea commented, "Miss Paula you are a super special person!!! Love ya." John was watching the video from Iowa and gave it a heart-shaped love.

Also today on Christie's Journey's Facebook page, Christie's great-aunt Lora's friend, Sherrie Hazen-Hansen posted: "Got my shirts today..." followed by an emoticon of a smiley face with red hearts for eyes. Several other people commented that they had received theirs today as well. Once again John gave out another heart-shaped love from Iowa.

Another friend, Amy Cooper Bodie posted, "Paul Bodie and I love you Christie Firth! So proud of how far you have come. God is AWESOME and answering everyone's' prayers! You keep resting and fighting. Continued prayers for you and your family." She included two pictures of her wearing her new T-shirt and holding up a heart symbol she was making with her hands. John thought to himself how blessed Christie was to have such good friends. Another heart was given out from Iowa.

27

July 7, 2019

Andrea entered the following onto the Christie's Journey Facebook page: "It has been a week since we came home to Texas. Christie is getting stronger and stronger, as her healing pain is showing up more and more."

Christie was tired. She took lots of naps each day. Andrea made sure her daughter didn't have to worry about Westin or household duties. Andrea took care of all of that. She also made things easier for Brian by being there. Brian was thankful he could go to work each day knowing that his wife and child had the best care they could have. Andrea also made sure Christie was taking her prescribed medicine as called for each day. She took six different pills in the morning and five at night to keep her heart working as it should. Andrea felt so fortunate that she had accumulated so much sick time at work that she was able to have all of this time off to take care of her daughter and still get paid. It was truly a blessing.

John had been back home in Iowa for a little more than a week now. Just about every day for the past four plus years, either on his way to work or to head into town in Washington for errands, he would pass a billboard not far from his house. The billboard is located on the east side of the Wayland Road with lots of foliage and trees around it. The message on the billboard reads, "Never will I leave you; never will I forsake you" (Heb. 13:5b). John thought about that verse like he never had thought before. He then said aloud in his car, "This is so true. Thank you, Lord." John went on to think, how many times had he driven by this billboard and never gave it much thought? He then realized and reminded himself that there are signs of God's work all around us every day. Sometimes it takes extreme circumstances to get people to notice them. John told himself he was going to acknowledge these signs, billboards, and other methods, man-made or from a higher power a lot better than he had been and he would also be pointing them out a lot more frequently.

Later in the evening John called Andrea to check in. "Hello, Dear, how's it going?"

Andrea replied, "Hi. It's going pretty good. Westin is such a good little baby. Christie gets tired pretty easily so she is resting a lot." John smiled and said, "They are lucky you are there. I miss you."

Andrea said, "I miss you too."

John asked Andrea about some mail they had and what bills needed to be taken care of. Not only was Andrea keeping a good watch on the Firth household in Texas but also had the Bain household in Iowa spinning right along. She told him that everything had been paid for online. John was glad to hear that and thanked his wife for having it under control.

John then started discussing Christie's situation with Andrea. "You know, I have never heard Christie complain through this whole journey. Never once. Has she said anything to you?"

Andrea said, "She has never said, 'Why me?' to me. I do know she is focused on getting better and that is her goal. I don't think she finds looking back or asking why to be helpful for her recovery. She has said to me that she is happy to be alive and is going to do what it takes to get better."

John smiled on the other end of the line and said to Andrea, "That sounds like our girl."

28

July 12, 2019

It's Friday! John had already put two full weeks of work in. It was good to get back to his regular routine. It was also nice to have a paycheck coming in again. While gone from work for thirteen working days, John's boss at the radio station, had made the decision for him that he probably would rather keep his vacation time than use it now and would probably rather use the time of absence as unpaid leave. John hadn't worried about any of that. His only concern was his daughter. Now that he had a weekend approach, and he didn't have to do any live remotes for the radio station, he was heading to Texas.

John had his clothes packed and ready to go at his house. All he needed to do was change out of his "work clothes," dress shirt, tie, dress shoes and slacks, and head on down the road. He had a twelve-hour drive ahead of him and it didn't matter. Soon he would be with Andrea, Christie, Brian, Natalie and Westin; and that is all that mattered to him.

John called Andrea and checked in. He could tell from the tone of her voice that she was tired and also happy he would be reuniting with all of them. Andrea said, "I want you to get here as soon as possible but I also don't want you driving overly tired. Can't you get a motel room tonight and then come the rest of the way in the morning?"

John replied to his wife, "You know I would rather drive late than get up early. I'll tell you what, I will drive as far as Farmington,

Missouri, tonight and then I will leave there in the morning. Does that work for you?"

Andrea was relieved that John had listened to reason and told her husband, "Yes, that works for me. Thank you."

John replied, "You're welcome."

Andrea said, "Text me when you get to the motel so I know you are there. You'd probably shouldn't call because it will be late and I don't want Christie or the baby to be disturbed."

John told his wife, "I will do exactly that. I love you."

Andrea said, "I love you too. Be careful."

John hung up the phone and continued down the highway in Andrea's Jeep toward Texas.

Christie was upset. Earlier in the day Natalie had asked her if she could get the mail from the mailbox. That's a big deal for a seven-year-old. Christie said of course she could as long as she looked both ways when she got to the end of the driveway to make sure no traffic was coming. Natalie promised that she would. Natalie got the mail. There was a lot of it. There were lots of cards from well-wishers. Christie had been opening the cards. They made her happy. Again she was overwhelmed by the messages and prayers of continued healing. There were also several cards that had checks in them. Then she opened the letter from Pafford EMS of Hope, Arkansas.

Inside the envelope was an invoice for her medical plane flight from Texarkana Airport to Cleveland Clinic. The invoice noted:

DESCRIPTION OF CHARGE	QUANTITY	UNIT PRICE	AMOUNT
AIR FIXED WING BASE RATE A0430	1.0	12500.00	12,500.00
AIR FIXED WING MILEAGE A0435	864.0	125.00	108,000.00
		Total Charges	120,500.00
	PLEASE PAY THIS AMOUNT		$120,500.00

Christie started crying. Andrea was holding Westin and Brian was watching television. Brian muted the television and asked Christie what was wrong. She couldn't speak. Andrea looked at her daughter and said, "Christie, are you all right?"

Christie held up the invoice and composed herself and then said, "This is the bill for my airplane flight to Cleveland. They say I owe $120,500.00!"

Brian didn't know what to say. Andrea asked Christie if she could look at the invoice. Andrea looked it over. "There has to be a mistake. We will have to call them on Monday and get this straightened out," Andrea said.

Brian handed Christie a tissue and she wiped her eyes. Christie looked at her mother, "I sure hope you are right, Mom. If you're wrong, what are we going to do?"

Andrea knew that getting upset right now was not the best thing for Christie. Andrea told Christie, "Try not to think about that right now. How about focusing on this little guy right here."

She smiled and looked down at Westin. He was content. Christie smiled and told her mom, "I'll try."

John left Farmington, around 8:00 a.m. He had slept a little longer than he had intended and was irritated at himself for that. He arrived at the Firth house around 2:00 p.m. He pulled up the long driveway to the house and he could see Andrea, Westin, and Natalie waiting and waving at him from the front porch. He was glad to be there!

Natalie ran from the porch to her papa and jumped into his waiting arms.

John smiled at his granddaughter and said, "How you doin' there, little lady?"

Natalie smiled and said, "Hi, Papa John! Momma is doing much better."

John still smiling, said, "I'm so glad to hear that! Now how are you doing?"

Natalie smiled as John placed her surefootedly back on the ground and she said, "I'm doing great! Can I carry your bag?"

John said, "Good! Yes you can."

Natalie smiled and said, "That will be a nickel, sir!"

John laughed and said, "Put it on my tab!"

Natalie scrunched her nose and said, "What does that mean?"

Papa John said, "Let me know how much I owe you later. I'm sure we will be adding to it."

Natalie said okay and ran in the house with John's bag.

John held his arms out and wrapped them around Andrea and Westin. It was good to be reunited. He kissed Westin on his little forehead and then gave his wife a kiss. John said, in his best Ricky Ricardo voice, "Lucy, I'm home!" Andrea chuckled and they walked into the house.

Christie was sitting on her recliner couch with a blanket on. Brian was right next to her and he got up and shook hands with John. Brian said, "Welcome back."

John responded, "It's good to be back. I thought I should come down here to give all of you a little break from Gigi and balance things out a bit."

All chuckled at that and John turned to Christie. Tears were starting to well up in John's eyes as he looked at his beautiful daughter while the thoughts of all that she and they had been through rushed through his head. Christie smiled and said, "Hi, Dad. Don't start crying. I'm doing good."

John nodded and said, "I'm just so happy that you are doing good." He gave his daughter a hug and was careful since she was wearing the LifeVest. John sat down on the other couch opposite the shared end table of where Christie was sitting and thought and thanked God for this huge blessing.

Christie asked her dad, "Did Mom tell you what came in the mail yesterday?"

John nodded, "Yes, can I take a look at it?"

Christie handed her dad the envelope which contained the invoice for the medical flight to Cleveland. John looked it over. He told Christie, "I don't see how they can hold you responsible for this whole bill. Your doctor deemed it necessary. You have insurance. You definitely met your deductible when Westin was born. This has to be a mistake."

Christie said, "I sure hope you are right."

The family had a good old-fashioned normal evening. Andrea and John played lots of rounds of Farkle with Natalie. All laughed and had a good time throughout the night.

At bedtime Christie said goodnight and hugged her dad. John was going to be back on the road by 6:30 a.m. so it would be a short night. Andrea would usually rock Westin to sleep in his nursery but John cut in for his chance tonight. John was sitting on the rocking chair in Westin's nursery holding him and giving him a bottle.

Andrea walked in and said, "I've got the monitor set up there so we can see him when you put him in his crib. We can hear him as well if he starts fussing."

John looked at his wife and smiled. "The only reason we will need that monitor tonight is if I need help with changing his diaper. I'm holding this little guy all night." Andrea knew there was no point debating the issue. She gave John a kiss on the cheek and said good night. John smiled and held his little grandson. He was where he needed and wanted to be. This way, hopefully Andrea will get a good night's sleep too. It had been quite a while since she had.

Morning came quickly. Westin only woke once during the night and John gave him a fresh bottle of formula and Andrea changed his diaper while John assisted. He kissed the sleeping Natalie on the cheek and left a dollar bill next to her piggy bank and then said and kissed his wife goodbye. He didn't want to wake up Christie and Brian so off he went. He had to be at work tomorrow morning at 7:30 a.m. so he needed to be on the road now to get back home at a decent time. He would be driving straight through. John was glad that he made the trip. He needed to be with Andrea and to see firsthand how Christie was doing. It was a very short visit but it accomplished a lot, and it felt good to be back behind the wheel of his Charger.

29

July 16, 2019

Lots of friends and family were receiving their The Beat Goes on... Christie's Journey T-shirts including Christie's Aunt Joni and cousins, Addy and Joe. Joni posted on the Christie's Journey Facebook Page: "We love you Christie! The beat goes on!" She included several photos of her and her children wearing their shirts. Christie smiled as she saw her aunt and her little cousins, Addy, age seven and, Joe, age four clowning around for the camera.

Time moves fast and slow together in sync in situations where a person doesn't know what is next and when things are supposed to happen. This is how it was for Christie and her family. Christie continued to get lots of rest. She also spent lots of time with her baby boy Westin. She was able to hold him and feed him while sitting down and Gigi was always close by to make sure she was comfortable. Christie was so thankful that her mother was there for her. "Mom, I am so grateful that you are here with me. I don't know how we could manage things right now if you weren't here. You are doing so much for us," Christie said with a thankful look on her face.

Andrea smiled. "Where else would I be? This is what mom's do for their kids no matter how old their kids are. Plus, I get to spoil these two grandkids of mine!" Andrea knew she could be in no other place right now. Not only did Christie and her family need her but also she needed to be with them.

With everything that has been going on, one other very important thing happening, was Westin was continuing to grow. It was time for his three month checkup. This had been delayed by a couple of weeks due to the overwhelming circumstances.

Andrea loaded up Westin and Christie into Christie's vehicle for their trip to Westin's pediatrician for his milestone checkup. When they arrived, Andrea parked the SUV in a handicap parking place out front of the building. Although not yet cleared to drive, Dr. Hayes had recently obtained the handicap sign for her vehicle and insisted that she take advantage of it and use the privilege because she needed it. Andrea hung the sign on the rearview mirror. Christie watched her mom place the sign on the mirror and said, "I don't like using that. I feel weird using it. I don't think I need it. People look at me as if I shouldn't be using it."

Andrea looked into the rearview mirror and told her daughter, "You do need it. Dr. Hayes would not have arranged for you to have it if he didn't think you needed it. And, since when have you worried about what other people think, young lady? If anyone has a problem with you having this handicap sign, then send them my way."

Christie smiled at her mother. "Okay, Momma Bear, whatever you say."

Westin's pediatrician, Christina A. Payne, MD, was impressed with how well he was doing and how well he responded to voices and other stimuli. She gave him a clean bill of health and encouraged Christie to keep doing what she is doing with him. Christie was very pleased to hear the good news. She also discussed what she has been going through and stressed her concerns about if there was a chance that Westin could have the same thing, even though she has been told that her situation was not genetic but a birth defect. Dr. Payne told Christie that she would schedule an echocardiogram for Westin to make sure all is okay. Christie thanked the doctor, "Thank you for doing this. I just want to make sure he is okay."

Dr. Payne responded with a smile, "I understand."

On the way home, the ladies decided to celebrate Westin's good checkup with a stop for lunch at a favorite restaurant of theirs on St. Michael Drive in Texarkana called TaMolly's. Christie really likes the chicken quesadillas there.

Andrea parked the SUV in a handicap parking spot near the building and placed the handicap parking sign on the rearview mirror. Christie got out of the back seat where she had been sitting next to Westin. Andrea proceeded to unhook Westin's car seat from its base and then grabbed his diaper bag. Christie was very self-conscious about this. How must this look to others that she is just standing there while her mom is doing all this work? Several people passed by during this process and Christie wondered how many people were thinking how selfish and uncaring she must be. She hated this feeling. She thought to herself, *Maybe I should have a sign or a T-shirt that says, "Don't judge me, I just had heart surgery."* The ladies made it into the building and were quickly seated. After their drinks were served and they placed their orders, Andrea started giving Westin a bottle. Several people sitting at tables around their table were cooing and smiling and making remarks on how cute a baby he was.

After they ate their lunch Andrea asked Christie if she would be okay while she made a quick visit to the restroom. Christie said, "Of course." Christie talked to her little baby and he smiled back at his momma. Christie reached for her Arnold Palmer (half tea and half lemonade), and accidently dropped it while bringing it over Westin. The little boy had drink and ice cubes all over him. Christie started to quickly pick up the ice cubes but she couldn't pick up Westin. The little baby started to cry and Christie was embarrassed that she spilled on him and even more self-conscious that she couldn't pick up her baby. The waiter came over with a towel and said, "You want to pick him up to wipe him off?"

Christie looked at the waiter sadly and said, "I can't."

Fortunately Andrea came out rather quickly and had assessed the situation while hurrying back to the table. "Oh, it looks like somebody got a little wet," Andrea said to Westin as she picked him up and took the towel from the waiter. She turned toward him and said, "Thank you, we are ready for the check." The waiter nodded and headed off to get the check.

Andrea said, "I think I will take him to the restroom and get him changed."

Christie said, "Okay, but I'm going with you."

The ladies got little Westin cleaned up and in a new set of clothes. They paid their bill and made their way home. Inside the car Christie was seated next to Westin on the backseat and said, "Momma's sorry for getting you all wet, little man. Will you forgive me?" Westin smiled at his momma.

30

July 18, 2019

Christie has continued to get stronger the past couple of weeks. She received the okay from Dr. Hayes to go back to work on a part-time basis. Today is Thursday and she is headed back to work. She thought by working today and tomorrow, and then having the week-end off, it would prepare her well for a full week next week.

Andrea asked her daughter, "Are you ready? You look great!"

Christie smiled at her mom and said, "I think I am. Are you going to be okay with the kids?"

Andrea smiled and said, "We will all be fine, and we will be waiting for you outside at noon." Although Christie was cleared to go back to work on a part-time basis she was not cleared to drive.

Natalie carried Westin's diaper bag to the car and Andrea carried Westin and got him secured in his car seat. Christie carried her purse and made her way to her car.

As they approached the Red River Credit Union, Natalie burst with joy. "It is so amazing to drop you off at work, Momma!"

She was smiling and Christie turned to look at her daughter and smiled and said, "Amazing?! Why is that. Honey?"

Natalie smiled and said, "Because you always drop me off at school and now, we get to drop you off at work!"

Christie smiled and said, "That is amazing, thank you!" Christie looked at Andrea.

Andrea was smiling. "Are you ready?"

Christie smiled at her mom and said, "Yes, I'm ready." Christie got out of the car and opened the back door and gave Westin a kiss and told him to be a good boy for Gigi. She then kissed Natalie and said, "I'll see you after while, young lady. Please be a good helper for Gigi." Natalie told her mother she would. Christie closed the door, waved and headed toward the building.

Christie's boss, Cindy, was waiting at the door to let Christie in. Since she had been gone for such a long period of time Christie's access card was no longer valid. Cindy smiled and gave Christie a hug. "Welcome back, young lady! I'm so glad you are back."

Christie smiled. "It's good to be back, thank you. Also, thanks again for everything you have done for me and my family. I really appreciate you bringing meals for my family up to the hospital. That was so nice."

Cindy smiled and said, "Don't mention it. All of us here just wanted to help."

Christie and Cindy made their way to Christie's office. They were slowed down several times by well wishes and hugs from fellow employees. A few tears fell. All were so happy to have Christie back with them.

Christie's friend, Cynthea, was happy and so relieved to have her friend back at work. Cynthea was smiling, "Girl, I'm so glad to have you back here. If you need anything you just let me know."

Christie thanked her friend. Christie went on to say, "I'm going to be working part-time from eight to noon. Hopefully everything will go good and I can get back to a full-time schedule soon."

Cynthea smiled, "It's so good to have you back! Remember, just holler if you need anything."

Christie said she would and Cynthea headed back to her desk.

Christie stood in her office. She looked around. She was trying to piece together in her mind the events of June 11th. There of course, were reminders all around her. The difference though, was that these reminders have had some changes to them since Christie was last here.

Christie noticed that the desk corners and shelf corners now had protective rubber around their edges. The huge floor safe that she had hit her head on now had these rubber protectors all around it. Christie's attention turned to the floor. There was a black rubber mat there that had not been there before. She looked at the mat, it was the kind that would be on a kitchen floor of a restaurant. She used her foot to turn the mat over. What she very quickly realized was that this mat was being used to cover the large stain of her blood from when her head was cut open from the safe as she bled from her right temple while lying there. Christie quickly turned the mat back over. She didn't want to see the bloodstain or even think about it. She also realized that if she dwelled on what happened and what the current conditions of her workplace were, that she probably wouldn't accomplish much.

Christie was logged back into the computer system of the credit union and she started back to work.

All went well her first part-time back. Christie was happy with how things went. It felt so good to her to be back at it. She was always an exceptional employee and her team was happy to have her back with them.

Andrea and the kids were out in the parking lot in Christie's vehicle waiting for her to get off work. About five minutes after noon Christie walked out the door with a smile on her face. Andrea and Natalie waved at her. Little Westin had fallen asleep on the way there.

Christie got in the car and said, "Hello."

Natalie said, "Hi, Momma! How was your work?"

Andrea was looking at Christie and said, "How did it go?"

Christie smiled. "It went pretty good. I remembered how to do everything. It was good to see and be with everybody. I am kind of tired right now. I think I could use a nap."

Andrea said, "Well close your eyes and we will be home soon. When we get home you can rest."

After arriving home, Christie went to bed and slept the majority of the afternoon. Andrea worried about her but knew that resting would be the best thing for her.

Brian got home a little after 6:00 p.m. He visited with Gigi and the kids for a little bit and then went into his bedroom to check on Christie. Christie had heard him in the other room and was awake and lying on her bed, propped up by some pillows. Brian smiled, "Hi, Babe."

Christie smiled back. "Hello."

Brian sat next to Christie on the bed. Then he realized his clothes were dirty from work. "Maybe I better shower and change first."

Christie shook her head no and said, "It's all right. Just sit here with me."

Brian continued to sit next to his wife.

"How did it go on your first day back?" Brian asked Christie.

Christie said, "It went pretty well. I was sure tired by the time noon rolled around."

Brian nodded and said, "That's what Gigi said, I suppose that should be expected. You know, you really have been through a lot."

The couple were holding hands.

Christie smiled at Brian and said, "Thank you for being here for me."

Brian replied, "You don't have to thank me for that. I love you. The only place for me is with you."

Christie said, "That's the same for me too."

Brian asked, "How is that LifeVest feeling on you?"

Christie gave an aching look and said, "I think I am developing muscles I never knew I had wearing this thing, but I am glad I have it."

Brian smiled. Christie then started telling Brian about different things that happened at work that day and how everyone was so nice to her welcoming her back.

"It was weird when I was first in my office alone. They had rubber pieces on all of the edges of my desk and on the shelves and even on that big old office safe. I felt like I was a little kid and they were 'babyproofing' my work station." She chuckled as she told him.

Brian said that he wished that they had "babyproofed" her office a long time ago, then maybe she wouldn't have hurt her head. Christie kissed her husband and he went off to shower and change. She got up and joined her mom and kids in the living room.

JOHN R. BAIN

Friday morning came quickly and Christie was ready. Andrea loaded up the kids and off they headed to Hooks, Texas, so Christie could go to work.

It was a good morning and Christie helped out several Red River Credit Union customers at the call center that day. Andrea and the kids picked her up at the end of her shift and they headed back home. Once again, Christie was tired by the time they got home. Andrea got her to eat a little bit for lunch and then she headed to her bedroom to rest. Like the day before, she slept the rest of the afternoon until Brian got home.

136

31

July 22, 2019

It had been a long night for Christie. She didn't sleep well and she was very uncomfortable. It was Monday morning and she was supposed to be at work at 8:00 a.m.

Andrea was about to get the kids ready for the drive. Her mother's intuition kicked in first though and she decided to check on Christie. She knocked on Christie's bedroom door. Christie responded, "Come in." Christie was lying on her bed and looked very tired.

Andrea asked, "How are you doing, Christie?"

Christie responded weakly, "I don't feel good, Mom. I'm tired and I haven't gotten much sleep."

It was hard for Andrea to hide the look of concern from her face. She said, "Well I don't think you need to go into work today. Let's plan on you resting and then see how you are doing tomorrow."

Christie agreed. She called into work and left a voicemail that she would not be in today but would do her best to be there tomorrow.

Tomorrow came. It was Tuesday. Christie was ready for work and Andrea had the kids ready to go. They were running early so they decided to stop at the Sonic in New Boston since it was on the way. Natalie had been extra good and a good helper to Gigi so she was excited to get her promised breakfast burrito. Christie had ordered a Diet Coke. She took a quick sip with her straw and quickly realized what she was sipping wasn't a Diet Coke. She wasn't sure what flavor it was but it definitely wasn't what she ordered. Christie got out of her car and walked up to the window and explained that she would need a different drink. The lady behind the glass apologized and gave Christie her Diet Coke. Christie smiled, thanked her, and walked back to her vehicle and got in on the rear passenger side. She sat down and didn't say anything.

Andrea looked at her daughter and asked, "Are you all right?"

Christie nodded and said, "Yes, just a little winded." She paused and then said, "I feel like I just ran a marathon."

Andrea said concernedly, "Christie, that's not normal. What do you think?"

Christie looked at her mom and said, "Mom, I don't know what is normal right now. I'm feeling better. Let's head onto work."

Andrea said okay and told Christie to try and relax. They headed onto the Credit Union Call Center.

Christie made it through her shift and was glad noon had arrived. She was very tired and feeling very sluggish. She didn't know what was going on and figured it was probably because she was out of practice working and that as she built up her stamina things would get better. She smiled as she exited the building and saw her own personal Uber with her mom, Natalie, and Westin waiting for her.

Wednesday came and Christie was still very tired and sluggish. Andrea suggested that it might be a good idea to take the day off. Christie told her mom, "I have to go to work, Mom. We've got bills to pay and I need the insurance. If I call in sick, they are going to think that I can't work. Then what?"

Andrea looked at Christie and said, "Let's see how today goes. If you aren't feeling better, then we are getting you into the doctor."

Christie begrudgingly replied, "Okay."

Andrea knew her daughter wasn't as she should be but went ahead and took her to work.

Noon came and Andrea and the kids were outside the Red River Credit Union Call Center waiting for Christie to come out. Natalie was looking out the window toward the door of the building. The door opened and out stepped Christie. Natalie was happy to see her. Christie got to the car and Natalie yelled, "Hi, Momma, how was your work?"

Christie looked tired. She sat in the rear passenger seat and put her head against the headrest. She said to Natalie, "Hi. Honey, it was good. Momma is tired so I don't think I should talk much right now so I can rest."

Andrea looked at her daughter, "I have texted Dr. Hayes. He wants you to come into his office this afternoon for a checkup."

Christie nodded at her mother and said, "Okay."

Afternoon came. Andrea had dropped Natalie off at her biological mother's home and proceeded to get Christie to Dr. Hayes's office in Texarkana. Andrea pulled up to the front of the building to let Christie out so she didn't have as far to walk. Andrea told Christie, "You go on in, Honey, and I will bring Westin in with me after I park. Just sit down in the lobby and I will get you a wheelchair."

"Okay," Christie smiled at her mother.

Christie walked into the medical office building. A woman was sitting at the front desk and asked Christie to approach.

Christie said, "Hi. I'm Christie Firth and I have an appointment with Dr. Hayes."

The woman replied, "Okay, Ms. Firth, you can go on up to Dr. Hayes's office."

Christie replied, "Thanks, I'm going to wait for my mom. She is bringing my baby boy in and is going to get me a wheelchair. I just had open-heart surgery a while back."

The woman looked at Christie and said, "Well if you just had heart surgery wouldn't it be good for you to walk for the exercise?" Christie didn't know how to respond to the woman. Fortunately Andrea walked in pushing Westin in his stroller. It was Texas hot outside and she had just pushed Westin quite a distance. Andrea looked at the woman at the desk and said, "Hi, I need a wheelchair for my daughter. She isn't feeling very well and does not need any more stress." The woman could tell that giving attitude to Andrea at this moment would not bode well for her and she pointed to a waiting wheelchair. Christie sat down in the wheelchair, and Andrea pushed Westin's stroller next to Christie. Christie grabbed the side of the stroller and then Andrea pushed her daughter to the doctor's office.

Christie, Andrea, and Westin didn't have to wait long for Dr. Hayes. They were met with a much-warmer reception from him. Dr. Hayes looked at Christie and said, "So you're not feeling very good right now, huh?" Christie nodded. Dr. Hayes continued, "Well we are going to see what is wrong and get you to feeling better."

Andrea interjected, "She has really been getting stronger these past few weeks until recently. She started back to work part-time last Thursday and did well both on Thursday and Friday, but was tired after her shifts. Once she was home, she would sleep a lot. Monday morning she wasn't feeling good and stayed home from work and rested all day. Yesterday wasn't much better, and I didn't want her to go into work today but she insisted that she go."

Dr. Hayes nodded at the worried mother and said, "Well it's important that she tried. She just recently had the surgery and we need to make sure we get things figured out so that Christie can get back to doing the things she is used to. Sometimes this is a trial-and-error process but I want to limit those trials and errors as much as possible. We will get this figured out."

Dr. Hayes decided to have Christie's EF checked. It is a good thing he did. Her ejection fraction rate was in the low twenties, similar to where it had been before her operation. Christie would have to be admitted to the hospital right away.

Fortunately, Dr. Hayes's office building is connected to Christus St. Michael Hospital. One of Dr. Hayes's staff wheeled Christie to admissions and Andrea headed off to Sam's Club with Westin to replenish his supply of diapers.

On the wheelchair ride to the hospital, the lady pushing Christie's wheelchair smiled and said to her, "You sure look young to be in the heart office."

Christie said, "Yeah, I'm 29. We found out that I was born with a defect in my heart. I'm pretty lucky to be here."

The lady's face came over with a look of recognition as she realized, "You're the miracle patient that everyone has been talking about. It's really neat to meet you. Most of the time we don't know what happens to people after they leave here."

Christie smiled and replied, "Yes, I guess I am. It's nice to meet you too."

Andrea called Paula Simmons and she met up with Andrea and took Westin home with her. Paula said, "Don't worry about this little guy, Ms. Andrea, we will take good care of him."

Andrea smiled, "I know you will, thank you so much, Paula."

Paula smiled and said, "Please tell Christie I hope all goes well for her. I will be praying for her."

Andrea said she would and Paula headed home with Westin, and Andrea headed back to the hospital.

Back at the hospital Christie called Brian. Brian answered and Christie told him that she was being admitted to the hospital and that her EF rate was not good.

He responded, "I'm on my way there, Babe. I know everything is going to be okay." Brian was nervous. Why was this happening to Christie again? Things were going so well. He was in his pickup truck. He headed toward Texarkana.

32

July 24, 2019

Wednesday evening. Christie was given diuretics; this was to help relieve her of excess water build up in her body. She was admitted to a regular hospital room, and Andrea and Brian stayed with her all night.

Andrea called John in Iowa to tell him what Christie was dealing with. John could not believe what he was hearing. He was just there a week and a half ago, and Christie was looking so good and doing remarkably well. "Did the doctor say why this is happening Andrea?"

Andrea responded, "He isn't sure why her heart is reacting this way but there are some issues with her blood pressure and she has some fluid buildup. They are going to run some more tests and take X-rays yet this afternoon."

John said, "Oh, Andrea, she has to be okay. Should I come down there?"

Andrea told her husband, "Let's see how things go over night and tomorrow morning and then you can decide if you should come."

John calmed down, "All right, but please keep me posted on everything." Andrea said she would and the husband and wife gave each other their love and hung up.

John was alone in his home in Iowa. He realized that he wasn't alone and asked God for his help once again, "Dear Lord, Christie is having problems again as you know. Please be with her and give her the strength, faith, and courage to get through this okay. Lord, we need her here with us. Please give her doctor and medical team all the knowledge, confidence, and skill needed to help her. Please look after Andrea, Brian, Natalie, Westin, and our entire family. In Jesus's name I pray, Amen."

A little later a nurse came into Christie's room. "Good afternoon, Christie, I'm here to take you for your X-rays."

Christie responded, "Good afternoon. Should we take this LifeVest off before the X-rays?"

The nurse thought for a moment and said, "No, it will be better to leave it on."

Christie wondered what the X-ray would look like and even if she would get stuck to the machine with all of the metal in it, with her LifeVest on.

Dr. Hayes walked in. "Hello, Christie. We're going to take some pictures of what's going on inside and see what our next steps will be." He turned toward the nurse and said, "We will need this LifeVest off. Go ahead and leave it off since she will be spending the night."

The nurse responded, "Yes, doctor."

Dr. Hayes turned to Christie and said, "I'll see you after a while and I'll let you know what we find out."

Christie thanked him.

Christie was somewhat irritated at the nurse not appreciating the uncomfortableness of the LifeVest and once she heard Dr. Hayes say it could come off, she motioned to Brian to help her get it off. Brian carefully worked around her IV and removed the LifeVest. Christie thought this was a wonderful feeling to have it off.

While Christie was having her X-rays, Brian and Andrea were visiting in Christie's hospital room. Brian said to Andrea, "I don't understand why this is happening to Christie again. I thought she was healing well."

Andrea tried to be reassuring to her son-in-law but she was having the same questions too. Andrea said to Brian, "The doctor said that her medicines may not be quite right now. They don't have many adult patients like Christie. Usually adults with heart problems have high blood pressure and other factors that Christie doesn't have. The medicines she has been on have been making her blood pressure too low. He also said that if they can't get a handle on it here, that they may need to send Christie to the heart center in Dallas."

Brian had been bowing his head while listening to Andrea. He looked up at Andrea and said, "I just want what's best for her. I want her to be well again. She doesn't deserve this."

Andrea nodded her head, "That's what we all want, Brian."

After Dr. Hayes had a look of the X-rays, he determined that he would be installing the defibrillator in the morning. Christie had another surgery ahead of her.

33

July 25, 2019

Christie had the best rest that she'd had in a long time. Not having to wear the LifeVest was such a blessing, even though she got out of bed several times throughout the night to use the restroom, it felt wonderful to have that LifeVest off. She was also visited several times throughout the night as the nursing staff checked the amount of fluid she was dispersing. It was a lot. Christie would find out that she relieved her body of three and a half liters of unwanted life-threatening fluid. Brian had slept well and Andrea had kept one eye open all night looking after her daughter.

It was early. A nurse walked into Christie's room pushing a scale along with her. "Good morning, Christie. I'm here to check your weight."

Christie looked at Brian and said, "I feel a lot lighter." Christie stepped onto the scale.

The nurse exclaimed as she double-checked her clipboard, "You have lost twenty pounds overnight, young lady. I bet you do feel a lot lighter."

Christie smiled at Brian and Andrea and said, "How's that for a quick weight loss?" They both smiled back at Christie.

34

July 26, 2019

Friday morning. It was almost time for Christie to have her defibrillator installed. Dr. Hayes and his team wanted to do some final checking before starting and scheduled an MRI. The MRI did not show any signs of reasons not to move forward. Christie would be having her defibrillator installed today.

Shortly after the MRI, Christie was whisked on her bed to the operating room after quick goodbyes to her husband and mother.

Once in the operating room, surgical personnel transferred Christie from her bed to the surgical table. Christie, lying down, looked up at the people standing around her and said, "Some of you look really familiar."

One of the men said, "We've met before when you were first here."

Christie nodded.

The anesthesiologist spoke to her, "Christie, I am going to give you some pain medicine."

Christie said, "I don't want the pain medicine because it makes me sick."

The anesthesiologist nodded and said, "I understand but the law says I have to give you at least the minimum amount."

Christie didn't want it but said, "Okay."

One of the masked personnel asked Christie if she liked country music. Christie said that she did. The next thing she heard was Garth Brooks singing "Friends in Low Places."

The procedure took about a couple of hours. During that time, Christie was awake during three quarters of the process. Dr. Hayes told Christie, "Christie, you are doing so well. You are quite a trooper. Most men that have this done are complaining quite regularly at this point of the process."

It was time to test the defibrillator. The testing would require Christie to be shocked by the device to ensure that it is working. The anesthesiologist did his job, and Christie was quickly under the sedation. The doctor activated the shock from the defibrillator. Christie's body jumped. Everything was functioning well.

Christie woke up shortly after.

Dr. Hayes smiled and said, "It all went well, Christie, I'm sewing up an incision and it's the shape of a cocktail."

Christie was groggy but happy that the procedure went as good as it did.

Brian and Andrea were recently informed that all had went well with Christie and she would be back in her room shortly. They were anxious to see her.

Moments later, two nurses arrived pushing Christie, who was resting groggily on her bed, and positioned her bed back in place. They smiled at Brian and Andrea. One of the nurses said, "She is a little groggy and that is understandable. The doctor would like her to rest a while, and we will evaluate how things are going and hopefully she can go home later today." That sounded good to Andrea and Brian and they thanked the nurses for helping with Christie.

Christie looked at Brian and her mom. She said, "I'm really sore. This hurts."

Andrea replied, "I will see if there is anything we can do to make things more comfortable for you. Maybe they can give you a little more pain medicine."

Christie shook her head no, "Mom, I don't want any more pain medicine. It makes me feel worse than the pain. I will just deal with it."

Andrea rubbed Christie's arm and said, "Okay."

While lying in her hospital bed, Christie started to assess her new situation. The defibrillator felt humongous and part of it stuck out into her left armpit. She thought, *This is going to take some getting*

147

used to. I don't think anyone who doesn't know it is there will be able to tell though. To get her mind off of the soreness, she started thinking about baby Westin. She smiled and closed her eyes.

Andrea went to the waiting room and gave John a call. She knew that her husband would have his phone right by him ready to receive the news. "Hi! How did it go?"

Andrea filled her husband in, "So with all of this she is pretty groggy right now and very sore. They said that she would probably be able to go home this afternoon."

John smiled. "That's great! How is she doing mentally?"

Andrea said, "She is taking all of this as she has been all along. She is amazing what she puts up with without too many questions. She trusts Dr. Hayes and is listening and doing what he advises. I think she looks at herself as in a position that this is a challenge, and she needs to go through some obstacle courses in order to achieve victory."

John listened to his wife and said to her, "She gets that from you, you know?"

Andrea smiled. "Ah, you two are just alike. I think she might get some of it from you too."

John smiled, "I love you."

Andrea replied, "I love you too. Now let me get back to her room."

John said okay and the grateful parents hung up.

Christie had a little lunch and was feeling less groggy. The pain from her defibrillator procedure was quite intense. That being the case, she could handle that much more if she got to go home today. Her wish came true around 4:00 p.m.

A nurse walked in and said hello to the trio.

She looked at Christie, "Are you ready to get out of here?"

Christie smiled and said, "Yes, ma'am."

The nurse opened up a plastic sleeve that held a sling in it. She started to adjust the strap as she fitted it around Christie's neck and left arm. "You will need to wear this sling for the first twenty-four hours that you are home. No lifting. None. Hubby and mom, please make sure she doesn't try to lift baby."

Brian responded, "We've all been real careful with that and will continue to be."

The nurse smiled and said, "Good. Now in a couple of days you are going to receive a shipment with an electronic device that will be bluetooth connected to your new defibrillator. It will send information via cellular to Dr. Hayes letting him know your heart rate and other information. This is a really neat machine because it can help your medical team know well in advance if you are going to or are experiencing any unwanted cardiac issues. The other thing you will receive is a scale that will also send your weight to the medical team so that we can make sure you aren't having any more fluid buildups or the like."

Christie took in everything the nurse had said and said, "Wow. I didn't even know all of that is possible. Is it hard to hook everything up?"

The nurse smiled and said, "No. All you have to do is plug it in when it arrives. The machines do the rest."

Christie was released from the hospital and rode home with Brian in his pickup truck, and Andrea followed in Christie's SUV. Christie told Brian, "It sure feels good to be with you."

Brian smiled and said, "It feels good to be taking you home."

The trio arrived back at the Firth home in Simms. They were all glad to be back. Andrea insisted that Christie go lay down on her bed while she got a light dinner put together.

While Christie was resting, Brian took advantage of the time as well and rested. Andrea used some of her time to post an update on the Christie's Journey Facebook page: "Latest update—Christie went to the cardiologist on Wednesday she wasn't feeling the best. They did an echocardiogram and found out her heart was weak again. So they admitted her. They changed her heart medicine twice until they found one that had better results. They gave her Lasix which helped her heart. Dr. Hayes put in a defibrillator today to help Christie. She is pretty sore from the procedure. But she got to come home. Thank you for everyone's love and support. Miss Paula kept lil guy the last 2 nights so we could stay with Christie. Thank you Simmons Family!!!"

Andrea noticed that Brandy Dastillon posted on Christie's Journey Facebook page; it was a picture of Brandy along with Robin Braley, Samantha Crump, Amy Walker Lindsey, and Jennifer Parkerson, gathered around a desk and all wearing The Beat Goes On Christie's Journey T-shirts. The caption read "New Boston Office supporting Christie today!" Andrea gave it a heart and fifty-seven other people gave it either a "like" or a "heart." In the comment section a gentleman named Stephen Potts commented, "Me too!!" Along with a picture of himself wearing his T-shirt. From Iowa, John commented to Stephen with a "Thank you." John wiped some tears from his eyes. He was overwhelmed by the generosity, concern, and love that so many people have shown for his daughter.

Lizbeth Macedo posted a picture of her and five others standing side by side wearing their The Beat Goes On Christie's Journey T-shirts with the caption "Phone center team checking in, praying for you Christie Firth" followed by a heart.

Christie's friend, Jessi Sisemore, posted a selfie sitting in her car wearing a The Beat Goes On Christie's Journey T-shirt as well with the caption "I've got on my team Christie gear too!!!" Team Christie has a lot of loyal members and they were out in force today.

Andrea followed up with another post "Thanks to Red River Credit Union Branches that wore Christie's Journey Shirts today!!" Andrea too was overwhelmed by so many people's generosity, prayers, and well wishes. She too teared up. She turned her head upward and quietly said, "Thank you."

Some time passed and Christie woke up and joined Andrea and Brian in the living room. Andrea had made ham sandwiches and got Christie to eat one. Brian had been in contact with Paula and she was on the way with Westin.

Brian asked Christie, "How are you doing?"

Christie smiled the best that she could and said, "It's real sore but I'm okay. I'm glad to be back home."

Brian said, "Do you want me to get hold of Paula and see if she can bring Westin home for us?"

Christie smiled, "Of course I do!"

Brian smiled back and said, "Good! Because I called her a little while ago and they should be here any minute."

Christie smiled. "Mom!"

Then she looked at Brian and said, "You're a real joker, Brian Firth!"

Every couple of minutes one of the trio would look out the front window at the driveway to see if Paula was pulling up. Andrea happened to be when she did. "Oh yay! Our little man is home!" She headed to the front door and went outside to meet Paula and Westin.

"Hello! It's so good to see you!" Andrea gave Paula a hug.

Paula said, "He has been such a good little baby. He definitely lets you know when he wants his bottle."

Andrea smiled. "He is such a good boy!"

Andrea unlatched the safety straps of the car seat and carried him inside. Paula followed. As they were walking in the front door, Brian was coming outside to get the car seat, stroller, and diaper bag. Westin traveled large. He gave Paula a hug and thanked her for all that she has done for them.

Inside, Christie was sitting on her couch. She smiled at her friend and thanked her for everything she has been doing for them.

Paula smiled back at Christie, "Don't even think about it, Christie. I told you I'm here for you and that's where I'm going to be. How are you doing, girl?"

Christie smiled at Paula and motioned with her left arm in the sling, "I'm okay. I'm really sore right now from where they put the defibrillator in me. I have to wear this sling for twenty-four hours and I'm not allowed to lift anything."

Paula said assuredly to her friend, "Twenty-four hours will zip by! I hope you are feeling better soon. Did they give you anything to take for the pain?"

Christie responded, "Yes, but you know me, I don't like to take pain pills if I can avoid them."

Paula nodded her head, "I'm with ya, but take them for the time being so you can have a little help feeling better until your body starts feeling better."

Christie told her friend, "Okay."

Andrea was holding Westin and he started to cry. Brian took Westin from Andrea to try and calm him down. He wasn't having any success. Christie said, "Why is my little man crying?" Brian walked Westin over to Christie and placed him on her lap while she held him with her right hand and arm. "You're okay. Momma loves you. Miss Paula takes such good care of you." The little baby relaxed and stopped crying. He knew his momma had him and he was content.

Paula said, "He could hear you talking to me and he wanted to be with you."

Christie smiled at her friend and said, "Yes."

35

July 27, 2019

Andrea was up early and posted onto Christie's Journey Facebook Page: "This is Christie's mom. I need to thank my work family. You are all amazing! I am so fortunate to be able to work with you all. From Illinois and New Jersey!!" John gave Andrea's post a heart and then followed up with a post of his own: "I also want to thank our son, Sean Bain. Son, you helped us all so much with your support and presence and good humor. Your mother and I are so blessed to have you and your sister as our kids. You make us proud every day!" Sean was looking at the page from his home in Blue Grass, Iowa, and gave it a like. He was happy and relieved things were coming together for his sister.

Michelle Kline, Christie's Uncle Joe's girlfriend, posted on the page from Davenport, Iowa, a picture of her wearing her The Beat Goes On Christie's Journey T-shirt and holding their two dogs, one in each arm with the caption: "We're bringing Christie with us to sweat… I mean shop and stroll…at the Bix today!!!" The Bix is the Bix Beiderbecke Memorial Jazz Festival that takes place in Davenport, Iowa, this weekend each year. It consists of lots of Jazz music, vendors, and a seven-mile run that brings thousands of runners to compete from not just the Midwest but also from around the world.

Christie woke up and joined her mother in the living room. Andrea was holding Westin and giving him a bottle. Christie smiled at her mom and touched her little boy on the side of his soft face, "Did my little man sleep good for Gigi last night?"

Andrea smiled and said, "He only woke up twice. Once he had a wet diaper and I changed him and then he went right back to sleep and the other time he was hungry."

Christie smiled at her mom and said, "I'm so glad you are here. Thank you."

Andrea smiled at Christie, "Here is where I'm supposed to be."

Christie was sitting on the couch next to Westin and Andrea taking care of some bills online via her iPhone. She checked her checking account balance to make sure she had enough dollars to cover the bills that she was taking care of. She was quite surprised! The balance was a lot more than she thought it should be. She then realized what was going on. A couple of weeks ago she gave Brandy Distillon and Jessi Sisemore the information needed to deposit money into her checking account. The ladies had followed through on the T-shirts and bracelets they had sold on her behalf. Christie was humbled and felt very blessed by this financial support that these two ladies made happen through their generous gifts of talent, time, and distribution. She showed Andrea the balance, "Mom, look at this."

Andrea said, "Wow. Is that from the T-shirt and bracelet sales?"

Christie teared up, "Yes, isn't it so nice of everyone that bought these shirts and bracelets? And how wonderful are Brandy and Jessi?"

Andrea smiled at her daughter. "They are great! We are so lucky that you have such nice friends. We are so blessed to have so many good people in our lives."

Christie smiled at Andrea and nodded yes.

On Tuesday, July 30th, Christie had a checkup scheduled with Dr. Hayes. Andrea waited in the waiting room and pushed Westin around the area in his stroller. Christie was feeling fine and Dr. Hayes was glad to see that she was. He wished her the best and sent her out to the receptionist to schedule her next appointment.

Christie reached the receptionist's desk, "Hi, I need to schedule my next appointment."

The lady behind the desk smiled and said, "Okay, let me call the calendar up on my screen and we will get you scheduled."

All of a sudden, Christie wasn't feeling good. She was getting warm and felt dizzy. She said, "I'm not feeling well and things are getting blurry."

The receptionist said, "Here, go sit down." She pointed Christie to a chair in the waiting room where Andrea and Westin were. Christie sat down. Andrea knew something was wrong, and she quickly went to her daughter and touched her forehead. She was clammy.

Christie said, "I don't feel good, Mom." The door opened and another patient came out. Before the door could close Andrea went through it and found Dr. Hayes. She told him, "Christie isn't feeling well." Dr. Hayes looked surprised and said, "Okay, I'll come see what's going on."

Andrea went back to the waiting room with Christie and Westin. Dr. Hayes arrived shortly after with a nurse. "So you're not feeling good?"

Christie nodded. "I'm dizzy and my vision is blurry and I'm hot."

Dr. Hayes grabbed one arm and the nurse the other. "Let's take you back and see if we can figure out what's going on."

Andrea followed pushing Westin in his stroller.

Once in the examination room, the doctor and nurse directed Christie to a chair and she sat down. Andrea, with Westin in his stroller, were close by. Christie looked around the room and then suddenly passed out. Andrea was frightened. "Should we get her a glass of water?"

Dr. Hayes looked at the frightened mother and calmly said, "We've got her." Dr. Hayes and the nurse slumped Christie down in the chair and elevated her legs. Another nurse came in with a glass of water. Dr. Hayes said to Christie, "Christie, can you hear me? Come on, girl, wake up."

Christie blinked her eyes and looked around the room. "What happened?"

Dr. Hayes smiled, "Well, I think with your lowered blood pressure that when you first left this room that you may have gotten up too fast and that caused all of this to happen. How are you feeling?"

Christie got her bearings and took another drink of water. "I'm feeling better now."

The doctor said, "Good. I'm glad to hear that."

After several minutes to make sure Christie was okay, the nurse got a wheelchair for Christie and wheeled her down to the car. Andrea had Westin already in his car seat and Christie joined him in the backseat. This turned out to be quite an afternoon. They headed to Simms so Christie could rest.

At 4:32 p.m. Andrea received a text from Dr. Hayes, "How's she feeling?"

Andrea responded, "Good. I noticed under other medications you are on prescriptions it says she is taking Toprol XL and she isn't, is that okay?"

The doctor replied back, "That's okay. I'll have them fix it."

Andrea texted back, "Sweet, thank you so much."

Dr. Hayes continued, "We fixed it here. Thanks."

Andrea typed back, "So glad you were there today."

Dr. Hayes replied, "Me too. Glad she's feeling better."

Andrea breathed a sigh of relief and was thankful that Dr. Hayes is so caring.

36

July 31, 2019

Andrea had been thinking about everything they had all been through the passed almost two months. The things she kept thinking about were; how blessed her family is to have the support of so many family and friends, and of course the love from God to guide them through this.

She posted on Christie's Journey Facebook page, "Huge Shout Out to Miss April Pierce Thompson. April stayed with Christie and us numerous nights in the hospital. Thank you!" Andrea also thought about her friends back in the Quad Cities: Jennifer, Peggy, Linda, Rose, Maggie, True Dee, Linda, Mimi, Patty, Brenda, and so many more. They all have been texting and calling to check in, sending their love and prayers. She doesn't know if they all truly realize how much their friendship and good wishes mean to her. They do know. Their actions of love, compassion, and loyalty prove that.

37

August 1, 2019

Christie is starting to feel better and continues to heal, but is nowhere near 100 percent. Her medications seem to being doing their job. Someone else doing their job was the United States Postal Service. The Firth house was receiving lots more in their mailbox than in the past.

Cards continued to be delivered from well-wishers as well as medical bills.

Christie has been fortunate in her adult life not to receive many medical bills because aside from what she is currently going through, she rarely had a doctor's visit except for yearly physicals and dental and eye care checkups.

Fortunately Andrea was there for Christie and between the mother and daughter each having a cell phone at their disposal, the two teamed up and made calls to different doctors' offices and to Blue Cross Blue Shield, in order to expedite as much as possible, all entities being on the same page and agreeing to what Christie actually owed. Christie thanked her mother many times for being there and helping her through all of this. "This kind of nonsense could make anyone go into cardiac arrest trying to figure it all out and to get it straight!"

Andrea smiled and gave her daughter a hug. "It's all going to work out, Christie."

Christie trusted her mom and smiled. Lingering in Andrea's mind was the fact that they still needed to get that medical plane bill settled.

Another major concern of Christie's was getting back to work. She is still not cleared to drive and doesn't know when she will be. She also knows that her mom can't stay here in Texas forever. She also struggles with the fact that her stamina isn't what it was before and she can't even lift her baby. How is this all going to work? "Mom, I don't know what I'm going to do about work. I need to have my insurance but right now I don't think I could even make it through a whole day."

Andrea looked at Christie assuredly. "Honey, you may not be able to go back to work. You might have to go on disability."

Christie looked at her mom and said, "I have to go back to work, I can't, I don't want to be on disability!"

Andrea knew that her daughter was upset enough at this point and decided to change the subject, "Let's focus on this beautiful little baby right now. Everything else will work itself out with time."

Christie smiled at little Westin. He looked up at his momma and smiled back.

On Saturday morning August 3, at 9:38 a.m., Andrea received a text from Dr. Hayes, "How has she been this week?"

Andrea texted back, "Three great days. Yesterday she actually lost two-tenths of a pound so I thought that was good with half dosage. This morning four-tenths gain so we will see. Energy level is okay."

38

August 6, 2019

John received a text from Christie at 3:02 p.m. It was a video of Westin lying on his back in his playpen. He could hear Christie giving him encouragement to turn over and to use his arms. He could also hear little Westin making some noises as he tried to maneuver. Westin reached for a little stuffed toy and pulled it next to him. The next thing that happened was Westin rolled himself over onto his tummy.

Christie and Gigi both said, "Yay!" at the same time and Westin lifted his head up and faced toward the camera. Christie typed a message to her dad below the video that read: "Westin is rolling over! We finally caught it on camera!"

John smiled as he watched the video and then typed back to Christie, "That's my grandson! Woohoo!"

Christie replied back a little later around 6:14 p.m. and texted, "Yeah I couldn't believe it when he did it in front of Mom and I. So amazing how he holds his head up now when he is on his tummy!"

John quickly replied back, "He's strong!"

Christie answered her dad, "Yes he is!"

John responded with a smiley face emoticon.

A couple of days later it was John's birthday. August 8. John was now fifty-three years old. He started his day off at work with donuts and his coworkers wished him a happy birthday and thanked him for sharing those donuts on *his day*. John received lots of "well wishes" and "happy birthdays" on Facebook, via text, and quick telephone calls.

At 10:32 a.m., he received a text from Christie, "Happy Birthday!!!"

He quickly replied back to his daughter, "Thanks, Honey!" John was in his car. He had just visited a client and signed them up for another three months of radio advertising. This was the third client in a row this morning that had renewed. It has been a really good day so far. He looked at his phone again and read Christie's text. The enormity of receiving those two words from his daughter sunk in. Tears welled up in his eyes and rolled down his cheeks. He kept staring at her text. He got a napkin out of the car console and wiped his face and eyes. He kept reading her text. The tears kept rolling. He kept wiping them and they kept coming. He was so overwhelmed with gratitude. He said, "Thank you Lord for letting Christie stay with us. Thank you, thank you. This is the best birthday present I could ever receive Lord, in Jesus's name I pray, Amen." After that, a calm came over him and he started his car and headed down the road. Even though it's his birthday, he still had more work to do.

On Saturday August 10th, Christie started stressing that she had a lot of pain in her left shoulder. She looked at Brian. "It's really sore."

Brian looked at his wife. "Is there anything I can do for you?"

Christie shook her head. "I don't think so. It hurts a lot though."

Andrea walked in carrying Westin. He had a fresh diaper and fresh clothes on. She asked Christie, "How are you doing?"

Christie looked at her mom.

Andrea could see she was in pain, "My shoulder really hurts."

Andrea handed Westin to Brian. "I'm going to get in touch with Dr. Hayes."

It was 12:50 p.m. The worried mother texted Dr. Hayes, "Christie's shoulder is in a lot of pain. Should we go to hospital?"

Dr. Hayes responded at 3:15 p.m. "What's wrong with it? Red? Sorry. I'm away at the lake. Poor cell coverage."

At 5:13 p.m. Andrea replied, "She said shooting pain up to her neck. The on-call doctor said to try Motrin between Tylenol."

Dr. Hayes quickly responded back, "What kind of pain? And can you send me a picture of the implant site? Any arm swelling? And does the pain happen more walking around?"

Andrea texted back, "The pain is the same walking. No swelling of the arm. Shooting pain from shoulder pain up the neck." Andrea followed with a picture of Christie holding her shirt down so that the implant site could be seen.

Dr. Hayes looked over the picture and replied, "Might just be rubbing up against a nerve. Not short of breath either? Try an ice pack on it? Looks okay to me. Not infected or bruising."

Andrea asked back, "So try an ice pack are you okay with Motrin in between Tylenol? Will that get better in time?"

The doctor replied, "It will. It's strange that it's happening this late though. Usually that's a first few days thing. Any chance she pulled a muscle? I'm fine with the Motrin/Tylenol."

Andrea told Dr. Hayes, "She told the nurse practitioner on Wednesday it was bothering her. She said it was mildly uncomfortable the whole time. Great, we will try ice and Motrin. Enjoy that lake. We go back Wednesday to your office. So far so good on meds. Big thank you!"

Dr. Hayes sent back, "Call me any time."

Andrea was grateful for Dr. Hayes instruction.

Christie felt a little better overnight but didn't sleep well. At around 10:15 a.m., on Sunday morning the eleventh, the pain arrived again. Andrea texted Dr. Hayes at 10:38 a.m., "Her pain just kicked in again and I put my Fitbit on her and her heart rate is up to 125. She didn't sleep again. Is there any pain meds she could have?"

Dr. Hayes was concerned and replied back, "Okay. Can you send us a transmission? Had the pain gone away?"

Andrea typed back, "She said it felt a little better last night. Sure I will send. But pain was stronger late she said thirty minutes not as strong."

Dr. Hayes asked, "What's her blood pressure doing?"

Andrea replied, "The blood pressure cuff doesn't work."

The doctor asked, "On her or anyone?"

Andrea typed back, "No, not on anyone."

The doctor texted, "Okay. I can call in some Tylenol 3 after church."

Andrea thanked the doctor, "Perfect TY, she said pain level 7. Would a muscle relaxer help??

At 12:25 p.m., Andrea received a text from Dr. Hayes, "What's her DOB and a pharmacy where you want it called in? Not sure. The device check looks completely normal."

Andrea replied back, "It's 2/23/90 Walmart New Boston. Please and thank you."

The doctor asked, "On New Boston Road or in New Boston?"

Andrea replied, "In New Boston."

Dr. Hayes said okay and called in the prescription.

The next morning Andrea received a text from Dr. Hayes. He was checking in to see how Christie was feeling. "How did that work for her?"

Andrea replied, "She said her shoulder is feeling much better. Should she continue for a bit w Tylenol 3?"

He replied, "Yeah. A few days maybe. It can be habit forming so as short as possible."

Andrea texted, "Sounds good. Westin has echocardiogram tomorrow."

Dr. Hayes texted back, "Okay good."

Andrea asked, "Is Christie released to drive? Is there a test to check to see if her sternum is healed?"

Dr. Hayes told Andrea, "My surgeon says just three weeks after the surgery. She should be set."

Andrea continued, "What about right side picking up baby."

Dr. Hayes answered, "Two months."

Andrea shared the information with Christie. Christie was frustrated and thankful at the same time.

39

Andrea drove Christie and Westin to Christus St. Michael Hospital in Texarkana for Westin's scheduled echocardiogram. Christie was nervous about what the upcoming procedure would reveal. She had been praying that all would be okay.

Christie was in the backseat with Westin. "Mom, what do you think they are going to find?"

Andrea glanced back in the rearview mirror to her daughter and said, "I'm hopeful they are going to tell you that he is perfectly fine. I feel that he is."

Christie looked at her mom's eyes in the rearview mirror and said, "I sure hope so."

When they got to the hospital Andrea hung the handicap sign from the rearview mirror of Christie's SUV. Andrea got the stroller out of the back of the vehicle and went around to Westin's side and unstrapped him from his car seat and placed him in the stroller along with his diaper bag. Christie was alongside her mother and talking to her baby boy. "You are such a good little man. Momma and Gigi are taking you into the hospital to get you checked out so they can tell us your heart is good and strong." Westin jabbered at his momma.

Christie, Westin, and Andrea waited in the examination room. Amy Carlyle, RDCS, entered. "Hello, everyone, I'm Amy. So, this must be Westin?" She looked at the happy little baby while his mother and grandmother looked on and smiled.

Christie looked at Amy, "Yes, this little one is Westin."

Amy smiled and said, "So we are going to do an electrocardiogram on Westin today. What are the reasons you have for concern?"

Christie replied to Amy, "Well, back on this past June 11th, I went into cardiac arrest at work. I spent quite some time here and then was flown to the Cleveland Clinic in Ohio for open-heart surgery to have an artery placed on the proper side of my heart due to a birth defect."

Amy started to have a look of recognition and excitement on her face while Christie was explaining her cause for concern about Westin.

Christie went on, "The doctors have told me that what happened to me was not genetic but a birth defect. I just want to make sure he is okay and if he isn't, I want to give him all the help he needs right now."

Amy blurted out, "Christie Firth! You are the Miracle! I was the one that gave you your first echocardiogram when you were first brought here by ambulance. It is so good to see that you are doing so well. We seldom ever find out what happens to patients after we see them and they go on."

Christie smiled. "Thank you."

Amy said, "You are so welcome. Now let me get started on checking out this little guy."

As Amy went through the procedure with Westin, he cooed and laughed as she moved the sonogram tool around his chest.

When Amy wrapped up, she said to Westin, "You did such a good job Westin!"

Andrea was holding Westin and Christie was looking at Amy with a look of desperation, waiting to hear what Amy had found. Christie said, "Did everything look okay?"

Amy responded, "Well, we will need to send the findings to Little Rock, and they will let us know in a couple of days."

Christie looked down at the floor, she was disappointed she couldn't hear the results now.

Amy added, "But, I'm not supposed to say anything, I know you've been through a lot. All looked good."

Christie turned and looked at Andrea and smiled. Andrea smiled back at her daughter and then looked down at Westin and kissed his little forehead.

Christie turned back to Amy, "Thank you."

Amy smiled and replied, "You are quite welcome. You'll get confirmation from us in a couple of days."

After discussions with Brian, Andrea, John, and Dr. Hayes; Christie came to the realization that she cannot go back to work at this time. Dr. Hayes did the proper paperwork for Christie to apply for disability. Christie was approved to go on long-term disability from the Red River Credit Union. She would continue to have insurance.

Two days later Christie received a telephone call relaying the good news that Westin's heart was the way it should be and doing well. She was so thankful to have this knowledge. It made her next task a little easier.

At 11:55 a.m., on August 15, John received a text from Christie's phone. The text was from Andrea and read, "We r at Christie's work packing up her office. I will call u later: baby sleeping on my lap."

John responded, "Wow. I bet that is rough on her. I'm glad you are there for her. I love you."

Christie, Andrea, and Westin were greeted by lots of well-wishers at the Red River Credit Union Call Center. They all doted over little Westin, and he ate up all of the attention. They also commented how much they were going to miss Christie there and hoped that one day she could come back. Christie said she hoped so as well.

While Christie was gathering up her personal items in her office, Andrea sat in a chair holding the sleeping Westin. She looked around the office and thought, *This is where it happened. Oh my, that is the safe she hit her head on.* She then looked down on the floor and saw the mat. She knew what was under it from when Christie had told her about the covered bloodstain, and she quickly turned her head. She saw the padding that was now installed around the safe and the different edges on tables and file cabinets. She wanted to leave. She was feeling claustrophobic. This is very upsetting. She wondered, *How was Christie able to come back in here?*

Christie spoke to Andrea and got her out of her thoughts, "Well, Mom, I have everything boxed up. I'm ready to go."

Andrea smiled at her daughter. "Okay, I'll put little one in his car seat and then we can get loaded up."

Christie looked at her mom. "I'm sorry I can't carry Westin or my stuff."

Andrea gave a reassuring look at her daughter and said, "You quit apologizing. It's not your fault. I know you would be the first to help if you could, so stop it."

Christie said, "Okay."

Andrea carrying the sleeping Westin in his car seat, along with Christie walking by her side, headed toward the door. Cynthea Vickery saw them and she volunteered to carry Christie's personal items to the car. The ladies graciously accepted her offer.

"Oh, girl, I'm going to miss you around here," said Cynthea to Christie.

Christie smiled at her friend and said, "I'm going to miss you too. But we can still get together."

Cynthea smiled as she put the box in the back of the SUV. "Oh, we will. That's for sure!"

The two friends hugged, and Christie got in the backseat with Westin and Andrea headed the vehicle back to Simms.

Later in the afternoon Andrea gave John a call. "Hi. How would you like to have some visitors?"

John asked his wife, "What do you mean?"

Andrea said, "Well, we picked up Christie's belongings today from the call center and she won't be going back to work for some time, and we have the car show coming up on Sunday the 18, and I thought we could get there in time for me to help with that and then I could go into work a few days next week."

John was excited, "Do you think Christie is up for all of that?"

Andrea had a happy tone to her voice, "We've talked it over. I do think she is up for it but we will have to have someone at our house with her and Westin when we are at work."

John interjected, "I will request Monday off as a vacation day, so that's covered. Who do you think we should ask? I think my aunt Linda would like to do it."

Andrea responded, "Yes, she is a good choice, and Christie always has fun with her. How about Michelle?"

John said, "Yes. I will get hold of both of them and see if they can do it. It's going to be good to have you back home."

"I'm looking forward to it but we will have to leave on Friday the 23 because there is a logging expo that Brian wants to go to in Hot Springs, and we are planning on meeting him there so Christie can attend. There are a lot of people that Brian does business with that will be there and it will be good for them to attend."

John said, "The twenty-third is our anniversary. Thirty-three years. At least we will be together for a little bit. When are you coming?"

Andrea said, "We will leave early tomorrow."

John said to his wife, "Well be careful and drive carefully. Please keep me posted on your progress. I'm looking forward to seeing you all. I love you."

Andrea said, "We will. I love you too."

The car show that Andrea referred to was the Paws and More Car Show on the Square in Washington, Iowa. Paws and More is the local no-kill animal shelter and the annual car show is their biggest fundraiser of the year.

John was excited and had to share the news with someone. He stopped into Glandon's West Side Service in Washington, Iowa, and visited with his friend, Craig Rembold. John and Craig were cochairing this year's event. Craig is a mechanic and also assistant fire chief of the Washington Volunteer Fire Department. John walked up to the service area of the garage. Craig looked out from underneath the Buick he was working on. "John Bain! Big John! What's the good word?"

John smiled. Craig always greets him like that when he stops by. John still smiling, says, "The good word, sir, is that Andrea will be at the car show this weekend and will be handling the registration table!"

Craig smiled, "Wow! She is coming home?"

"Yes she is! She is bringing Christie and my grandson with her. They are going to stay next week and Andrea will be going back to work while she is here. They will go back to Texas at the end of next week."

Craig smiled and Terry Glandon, John's friend and owner of the garage joined the conversation, "That is great news!"

John turned to Terry. "It sure is. I'm really looking forward to it."

Terry asked, "How is your daughter doing?"

John said, "For everything she has been through, she is doing pretty good. She has a long way to go though. She hasn't been cleared to drive and she isn't supposed to lift anything, including her baby, and she is currently on long-term disability from work. But even with all of that, she is progressing and we are all so very grateful. God is Good!"

Terry and Craig nodded in agreement at their friend.

40

August 16, 2019

John received a text from Christie at 12:22 p.m., "We are in Farmington."

John replied, "Woohoo! Keep on keeping on." John noted that the trio was making good progress. According to his Google Maps app on his iPhone they should be at his house in four hours and twenty-seven minutes. He was excited! If all goes well, that will have them arriving around 5:00 p.m., or a little later.

John finished up his work day and had his vacation day for this upcoming Monday approved. He was looking forward to his three-day weekend with his family.

Another thing he was looking forward to, was delivery of his new zero turn lawn mower he recently purchased from one of his clients. It was scheduled to be delivered around the same time as the Texas trio were to arrive. John chuckled at himself as he thought how everything always happens at the same time with him. He equates it to the man on the stage with all kinds of poles with dishes spinning on top of them. Everything is going good until one of the plates on the opposite end of the stage starts to wobble and the man has to run to the plate and get it spinning again and while doing that, sees another plate wobbling on the other end. He is used to that and so is Andrea.

It was 5:20 p.m., John was looking out the kitchen window of his house toward the driveway. Who was going to get there first? His family or his new lawn mower? Suddenly he sees the front end of Andrea's Jeep coming up the road and signaling a turn into his driveway. John headed out the front door and waited for his family to pull up.

Andrea parked her car and John opened her door. "Welcome home!" He kissed his wife.

Andrea said, "Thank you!"

"How was your trip?"

Christie interjected from the back seat, "It was long!"

John opened his daughter's door and hugged her when she exited the car. "You are looking really good, Christie, welcome back!"

Christie smiled at John. "Thanks, Dad."

John looked into the vehicle. "Where's my little buddy?"

Westin was moving his arms and legs. He was ready to be out of his car seat. John unhooked the straps and lifted his grandson out of the car. "Can you say 'Papa'? Papa loves you. Westin, you are my good boy!" Westin smiled at this crazy man as John carried him in the house.

After John and Andrea had Christie and Westin settled, they unloaded her car.

John asked, "How is she doing?"

Andrea looked at her husband and said, "She is still weak but getting stronger. She needs lots of rest. She is really something. I'm so proud of her."

John looked at his wife and held her shoulders, "I'm so proud of you. We would not have been able to go through all of this without you." Andrea smiled and John hugged her. She said, "I'm just so happy she is getting better."

A few minutes later a truck pulling a trailer with John's new lawn mower on it turns into the driveway. John goes outside to greet Larry Fred Gerling. "Hi, Larry!"

Larry waves at John. "Hello, John! I bet you are glad to see this arrive."

"Yes, sir, I sure am!"

"Well let me get this unloaded for you."

"Sounds good!"

In the meantime Andrea had also exited the house carrying Westin followed by Christie. Larry Fred's wife, Patti, was with him and introductions were made. Christie looked so good that they were both quite surprised at how recently Christie had undergone her surgery.

While Andrea and John were visiting with the Gerlings, Christie got on the new lawn mower and started it up. The next they see is this young lady with her ponytail, flopping behind her, driving the lawn mower all over the front yard. Even though it was a lawn mower, the wind hitting Christie's face felt so good to her. It was freedom! She had not been this much on her own for a very long time. It felt so good. She smiled.

Christie continued smiling as she pulled the lawn mower back to where she had commandeered it. John took a couple of pictures of her on it. "What in the world do you think you are doing, young lady?"

Christie smiled. "Dad, we have one of these zero turns at home, and I wanted to see how yours compared?"

John smiled, "Well?"

Christie smiling, told her dad, "It's a nice one!"

Patti turned to Andrea. "When did you say she had that surgery?" They all laughed.

Saturday came quickly. John called his aunt Lora early that afternoon, "Are you up for some visitors?"

Lora responded, "Well, yes, but I have to leave for work around two thirty."

John said, "Okay, we'll be right over for a short visit. That will work good for all of us."

John, Andrea, Christie, and Westin loaded up and headed next door to the family farm.

Lora, Donald, and Tom Bain are John's father's siblings. They live together on the Bain family farm. The group arrived and John knocked on the door and entered, "Anyone home?" The three were sitting around the dining room table. They were pleasantly surprised at how well Christie looked. Christie gave her two great uncles and her great aunt a hug. John was holding Westin.

He said, "Everybody, meet my grandson, Westin!"

They all said, "Hi, Westin!"

Lora turned to Christie, "How are you doing, Christie?"

Christie smiled. "I think I'm doing pretty good. I'm not supposed to lift much but I get tempted once in a while with Westin. I get tired quite often too."

Lora said, "Well that is understandable to get tired. You look very good."

Christie said to Lora, "Thank you."

The family visited for a while and then it was time for Lora to head to work. Lora said, "I hope you don't mind if I stop by from time to time this week to get my 'Westin Time'."

John, Andrea, and Christie said that would be fine and she was more than welcome to.

The foursome went back home and Christie and Westin took a nap. John and Andrea relaxed and enjoyed the quiet.

Later that afternoon, the Bain household received a visit from Sean. He entered the house and all gave him a welcome.

Sean hugged his mom. "Welcome home."

Andrea smiled and said, "Thank you. Have you gotten taller?"

John interjected, "Maybe you've gotten shorter." His wife stuck her tongue out at him.

Christie was in the living room sitting on the couch holding Westin.

Sean saw his sister, "Hi, Christie. How are you doing? You look good."

Christie looked at her brother, "Hi, Sean. Thanks, I'm doing pretty good. I'm getting stronger."

John added, "And, she isn't supposed to be lifting Westin or anything else so if you see her start, make her stop."

Sean looked at his dad and saluted, "Yes, sir!"

The family laughed.

Sean sat down next to Christie and held his little nephew. Westin seemed happy in Uncle Sean's arms.

John's alarm went off at 5:15 a.m. on Sunday morning. It was car show day. He showered and grabbed a couple of hard-boiled eggs and some juice and had a quick breakfast. He was trying to be as quiet as possible so as not to wake anyone else up. Andrea would get up a little later and meet him at the town square in Washington.

John headed out to his garage. His 1970 Dodge Charger, The General Lee, a tribute car to his favorite childhood television show, *The Dukes of Hazzard*, was waiting in its bin looking good and ready to go. John opened up the garage door. To his surprise it was raining hard. John thought to himself, *Oh no, we don't need this today.*

John called his cochair of the event, Craig Rembold. "Can you believe this rain?"

Craig replied, "It's crazy. It seems to be letting up here. I'm already at the square setting up the barricades."

John said, "Really?! It's raining cats and dogs here right now. It's a real gully washer. I'll tell you what, I'll wait here for a little bit until it dies down some and then I'll head on up. Leave me a little work to do for when I get there."

Craig said, "Copy that. I'll see you in a little while."

After a short time the rain let up. John thought to himself, *Why did I even detail this car? I hate to see what it looks like by the time I get to town.* John started the hot rod up. It sounded great! He smiled and backed the car out of the garage and said out loud, "That's why!" He headed up the road to Washington and hoped for the best regarding the weather.

John arrived and parked his car in the display area of the event where the non-judged cars are parked since his car would not be eligible for a chance at a trophy today because he was one of the officials of the show. He joined Craig and they finished placing the barricades.

Craig said to John, "Well what do you think? Are we going to have a car show today?"

John looked at the skies. "Right now I would say there is a 50/50 chance. The bad part is, if it looks like it does now, people aren't going to want to bring their cars out. And, if it clears up here and this stuff goes somewhere else nearby, they won't get them out either. It's not looking good."

Craig shook his head. "No, it's not. I want to have a car show today."

John smiled at his friend. "Let's hope Mother Nature wants to have one today too."

Andrea arrived about a half hour later. Craig was happy to see her. It had been quite a while since he got to tease Andrea. "Well hello, stranger, welcome back!"

Andrea smiled at Craig, "Thanks, it's good to be back."

Craig asked, "How's Christie, is she doing well?"

Andrea said, "She is doing much better and is back at our house with her baby and our son is there with them too."

Craig smiled. "That's good to hear. So, are we going to have a car show today?" Before Andrea could answer, a loud rumble of thunder followed by a flash of lightning and another rumble of thunder along with the start of a monsoon came from the sky. They hurried to the band shell for shelter.

Around 8:30 a.m., Sheila Hanson, volunteer board president at Paws & More Animal Shelter arrived. She has had a very busy week tying up loose ends to help get her son, Logan, ready to leave for college today as well as everything involved with this car show.

Sheila smiled. "Good morning!"

John, Andrea, and Craig replied, "Good morning!"

It was still raining. John introduced Andrea to Sheila. The two ladies shook hands.

Sheila said, "It's not looking very good for today is it?"

John and Craig shook their heads and John said, "No, it's not. We have registration scheduled until 11:00 a.m. and right now, as you can see, there are about five cars here. Usually all of the power parkers are here by now. It's not looking good."

Sheila agreed. "I don't know what we should do."

John said, "Unfortunately with what we are being dealt with by the weather, I fear that even if it stops raining here, this weather system is going to be unleashing around us and that will keep the people away." Sheila and Craig agreed.

John contacted his friends that were coming to the event from the Quad Cities area and beyond to let them know that things weren't looking good. Sparky Bentley thanked his buddy for calling. He mentioned that he and his wife, Brenda, were about to head out, even though it was raining up in Camanche, Iowa, but would now be staying home. John then contacted his friend, Steve Simmons, from Davenport, Iowa, to let him know. Steve thanked him and said that his wife, Barb, would be happy to get to sleep in. Andrea had called Rose Reasor and her husband Jerry, from Moline, Illinois, they were already on their way so Rose said that she would be seeing Andrea soon.

The morning rolled on with on-and-off rain. At 10:30 a.m., it had stopped raining. With registration over at 11:00 a.m., Sheila, John and Craig decided to cancel the show for today with hopes of trying again in September.

Sheila said to John, "I think we should cancel. What do you think?"

John agreed. "Yes, we aren't going to have good participation today and that isn't good for Paws & More. I think we should postpone and try again next month."

Sheila sighed. "Maybe I'm getting a chance to spend a little more time with Logan today before Chris and I send him off to Millikin University."

John smiled. "I think that makes a lot of sense, Mom. Now go home and spend some time with your son before he goes. Andrea and I have family at the house and it will be good to have the extra time with them too."

Sheila smiled and thanked John.

Last week when it was decided that Andrea, Christie, and Westin would be coming to Iowa, Andrea reached out to Patty Hepner, John's cousin Doug's wife, in Kewanee, Illinois, to come and visit with Christie and Westin while John and Andrea would be at the car show. She thought this would be a nice relaxed time to visit. Patty agreed and was looking forward to seeing Christie and meeting Westin.

The Hepners arrived along with their two daughters, Sarah and Katie. The girls grew up with Sean and Christie and were looking forward to seeing firsthand how their cousin was doing and to meet her new baby. The two families are very close. The Hepners even traveled to Arkansas and Texas a few years back for Christie and Brian's wedding.

Doug looked at Christie and said, "Hi, Christie. You look great!" Christie smiled. "Thank you."

Patty, Sarah, and Katie all gave Christie a hug.

Doug went on, "You know, I've been seeing pictures of Westin and he sure looks like your Grandpa Russell."

Christie smiled. "Yes, he definitely resembles this side of the family."

Patty asked if she could hold Westin and Christie said, "Of course." Westin was very happy and smiled at Patty. Sarah and Katie started catching up with Christie and Sean chimed in as well.

Jerry and Rose arrived at the square. Andrea and John thought it would be the right thing to do to offer lunch at a local restaurant after Jerry and Rose coming so far. The Reasors accepted and Andrea called Christie to let her know they were going to lunch. Christie asked if they should join them and Andrea said of course.

Andrea loaded up in her car and John in the General Lee as Jerry and Rose brought up the rear in their 1960 Pontiac Starfire "rat rod" and headed over to Unc & Neph's.

By the time all arrived at Unc & Neph's for lunch the group had expanded to twelve people. John's sister Joni had been camping at the family farm and she and her two children, Addy and Joe, joined the group. John, Sean, and Doug pulled some tables together and all got settled. Unc & Neph's was busy that day so adding another eleven orders, Westin wasn't participating with the menu, took some time to get made and served. The group had a nice and loud visit. John thought to himself, *How many plates have fallen off the poles today?* He smiled and enjoyed the joyful noise.

It was going on 2:00 p.m. Sean sent Lora a text saying they were on their way home. Lora got ready and headed over to John and Andrea's house. When she arrived no one was there yet so she waited in her car. Suddenly she sees John pulling into the driveway in the General Lee followed by Andrea and then Jerry and Rose. Then here came Sean's vehicle and one other and then her niece Joni's. Lora thought to herself, *This is crazy. They don't need me here right now. This is just too many people.*

Lora stayed in her car and was getting ready to go back home. Joni walked up to her and said, "What are you up to?"

Lora responded at her niece, "Oh, I am just taking care of something on my phone."

Joni brushed it off and said, "Okay, I'll talk to you later."

A couple of minutes later Sean came out to Lora's car, "Hi. Whatcha doin'?"

Lora said, "There are just too many people in there. I'll come back some other time." Sean looked at his great-aunt and reassured her, "It's okay there is room. Come on in."

Lora begrudgingly obeyed Sean's invitation.

Inside the house the people were in different groups throughout the kitchen, living room, and dining room. Lora found a seat on the couch next to Christie and Westin.

Lora said to Christie, "I'm sorry, I can come back later. I don't want to add to your stress level."

Christie told her great-aunt, "It's okay, besides you need to get your 'Westin Time' in today."

Lora smiled. "I guess you are right. Let me hold that baby!"

A couple of minutes later, Gary Bain, Lora's other brother stopped in. He and his wife, Loree, had been concerned for Christie, and how she was getting along and since he had been next door at the farm he decided to stop by.

John answered the door, "Hi, Uncle Gary, come on in."

Gary said hello and entered the house. Christie saw her great-uncle and smiled and said hello. He asked how she was getting along and she gave him an update. He was glad that she was doing so well.

They started looking and talking about Westin when Doug said to Gary, "If we gave him a little cigar he would look just like Russell!"

Gary looked at his great-nephew and said, "Russell smoked?"

John interjected, "Yes he did."

Gary seemed surprised to hear that about his brother. "I guess I didn't know that."

A little more time went on and it was evident that Christie was getting tired. It was also evident that little Westin was too. Andrea took him into a far bedroom to get away from the activity so he could rest. Everyone departed and the house got quiet.

John said to Christie, "Wow, you have a lot of people who care about you, young lady."

Christie yawned and said, "Yes. I'm tired. Do you mind if I go lay down for a while?"

John looked at his daughter and hoped that the organized chaos had not been too much for her. "No, by all means go get some rest."

Christie hugged her dad and went down the hall to her room to lay down.

Sean looked at his dad, "I'm going to go lay down too."

John smiled. "Okay, Champ." John looked around the room and listened to the quiet. He looked up and said, "Thank you."

41

August 19, 2019

John held Westin all night long. His grandson slept peacefully most of the night. John spent a lot of time looking at Westin and thinking what a perfect little baby he is. He also thought about Sean's visit here on Saturday and Sunday and how good it was to see him interact with Christie and to get to know his little nephew better. John could also tell how happy Andrea was to be reunited. And then all the people that ended up here at the house on Sunday, it was crazy wonderful! John felt like things were getting better and maybe even, he dared to hope, having some sense of normalcy. He acknowledged how truly blessed they all are.

Around 2:00 a.m., Westin woke up fussy. He had a wet diaper and was hungry. Andrea was in their bedroom. It is the first time she has gotten to sleep in her own bed since June. Andrea could hear Westin fussing over the monitor. She joined John in the living room. Andrea smiled. "Is our little man hungry? Let's get that diaper changed." Andrea laid Westin on the living room floor on top of his blanket and proceeded to change him out of his wet diaper. John distracted Westin and kept him from crying. Both grandparents remember getting up from the floor a much easier task when their kids were this age compared to now.

John picked up the fussing Westin from the floor and sat down with him on his recliner. Andrea returned from the kitchen with a fresh bottle. "Here you go." John took the bottle from Andrea and proceeded to feed Westin. Westin was happy and settled right down.

Andrea said to John, "Do you want me to take over?"

John shook his head no to his wife, "No, Honey, I will take it from here. You have to get up and go to work in a couple of hours. Go get your rest."

Andrea kissed John and headed back to bed. John quietly sang "You Are My Sunshine" to Westin.

Four in the morning came quickly. Andrea hurriedly got ready for work and was out the door by 4:30 a.m. She had an hour and a half drive ahead of her.

On her way to work, Andrea thought about how long she has been gone and what would be her first task of the day once she got there. She was glad to be going back. She missed her friends and coworkers and also has been missing the actual job too. Most importantly though, she really appreciated how blessed she has been to be able to be with Christie during all of this.

Back in Wayland, John was having a fun time with his grandson. He was so happy to have Andrea, Westin, and Christie with him. Westin rolled around on the floor and grabbed at some of his baby toys. The noise makers not only stimulated Westin but also Papa John seemed to enjoy them too.

Christie awoke and joined John and Westin. "Good morning."

John looked at his daughter, she looked great, "Good morning, Honey, did you sleep good?"

"Yes, how did you do with this little boy?" She smiled at Westin and rubbed his little chest. Westin smiled at his momma.

John told her, "I think we did pretty darned good. He likes his papa to hold him. We had all kinds of good talks and we sang songs."

Christie smiled. "Oh did you now?"

Andrea arrived on time at the Rock Island Arsenal in Rock Island, Illinois. She parked her car and made her way into her building. Andrea approached her desk. Things were in the same place as they were when she left at the end of the day back on June 11th. It felt good to be back. Even though this was going to be a short stint back to work, working here in the office today, Tuesday and Wednesday, and working from home on Thursday, she really needed to be back and it felt right and normal.

Throughout the day Andrea had lots of coworkers stop by her desk to welcome her back and get the latest update on Christie. One of the earliest visitors of the day was Andrea's friend, Jennifer Vernon. Jennifer approached Andrea's desk with her arms outstretched. Andrea stood up and gave her friend a hug. Both women were smiling. Jennifer said, "Welcome back! You look great! How are you doing, Sweetie?"

Andrea smiled at her friend, "I'm doing good. It's so good to see you. I've missed you."

Jennifer replied, "I've missed you too. It's just not the same around here without you."

Andrea responded to her friend, "Thank you."

Back in Texas, Brian was busy at work on a job site. There were a lot of trees to cut on this hilly acreage. Brian took a break and visited with his dad, Butch. "I just want to thank you again for all of your help while Christie was going through her surgery and stuff."

Butch looked at his son and said, "I'm glad we were able to help. I'm also so happy that Christie is going to be okay. You've got a real good one there."

Brian nodded at his dad. "Things are going to be a little different for a while but she is getting stronger every day."

Butch said to Brian, "You are lucky Ms. Andrea has been able to be down here with her."

Brian told his dad, "That's for sure."

The two men talked about their next plan of action and which plot they would be attacking next.

Brian then asked, "The logging expo is coming up this weekend in Hot Springs. Christie and Westin are coming back down with her mom, and I'm going to pick up Natalie and we are all planning to meet there. Would you be able to watch the dogs while we are gone?"

Butch responded to Brian, "Isn't that going to be a lot of walking? How is Christie supposed to do that?"

Brian said, "Yes, it's going to be a lot of walking but Andrea has reserved a wheelchair at the hotel that we can use for Christie at the expo."

Butch said, "That is good thinking. Yes, I'll look after your dogs."

Brian's phone rang. It was Christie. Brian told his dad he needed to take the call and walked away. "Hello."

Christie sounded strong on the other end, "Hi, Babe. How is your day going?"

Brian smiled. "Hi. It's going good. How are you and Westin doing? I miss you."

Christie replied to her husband, "I miss you too. We are doing good. Dad is spoiling Westin right now. He is telling him all kinds of stuff and Westin eats it up."

Brian said, "That's good!"

Christie replied back, "We will see about that. Did you get a chance to ask your dad if he could watch the dogs?"

"Yes I did and he said that he could."

Christie smiled. "Good! I didn't want you to forget to ask."

"Thank you, dear."

Christie said, "You're welcome. Now be safe and get back to work. I love you."

Brian gave his wife a "can do" response, "I will! I love you too."

At lunch time, John asked Christie if she was hungry. "Well, young lady, what are you fixing us for lunch?"

Christie smiled at her dad and said, "Wait a minute, I thought I was supposed to be taking it easy? Shouldn't it be what are you fixing me for lunch?"

John smiled and nodded, "How about some French toast and scrambled eggs? Or I could mix up some tuna salad?" Although all were good choices, Christie really wanted to get out and about for a little while. John interjected, "Would you like to go to town for some Mexican food?" Christie told her dad that sounded good. She got Westin changed and they headed into Washington for lunch at Mi Pueblo Real.

While having lunch at the restaurant, Westin fell asleep in his car seat. He was positioned next to Christie on her side of the booth. John sat across from them and enjoyed being with both of them. "You know how fortunate and blessed I feel, Christie?"

Christie looked at her father and tried not to be embarrassed. "Dad, I know."

John continued, "Well, I want to make sure you know. I love you. I love that little boy next to you and that little girl that is down in Texas right now and even that lug you are married to. We are so fortunate to have a strong family and the good Lord has truly blessed us. We have won life's lottery."

Christie smiled at her dad and stuck out her tongue at him. John laughed.

Early evening came and Andrea was back home from her first day back at work. She was tired but it was a good tired.

After supper, John's brother, Joe, along with his girlfriend Michelle stopped by. They are staying the night in their camper that is at the family farm next door, and Michelle is going to stay the day with Christie and Westin tomorrow while John and Andrea are at work. Aunt Lora also stopped by to get her "Westin Time."

Christie's Uncle Joe was so glad to see his niece. He has been so worried about her. Christie gave her uncle a big hug. Joe smiled. "How are you doing, Christie?"

Christie smiled at her uncle. "I get tired easily but other than that my strength is coming back, and I feel pretty good."

Joe told his niece, "Well don't rush anything. You look great!"

Michelle Kline looked at Christie and smiled and gave her a hug. "Christie, it is so good to see you. We are so proud of you. I can't wait to spend the day with you and this little guy tomorrow!"

Christie smiled. "Thanks for giving up your day to hang out with us."

Michelle smiled. "I can't think of a better way to spend it."

42

August 20, 2020

Tuesday came and Andrea headed back to Rock Island for work. John was up by 6:00 a.m. to get ready for his work day. Westin was sleeping so he quickly got ready in hopes that he would continue sleeping just a little bit longer as to not disturb Christie and interrupt her rest.

Michelle Kline arrived around 7:00 a.m. She was ready. She had her coffee brewed and felt she could tackle anything. John visited with Michelle while he ate his breakfast.

John looked at the sleeping Westin as he was walking out the door. Michelle said, "Don't worry, everything will be fine. If I need anything, I will wake up Christie and we've got both yours and Andrea's number and your brother is close by at the farm."

John smiled. "I know. I just wish I could stay with the little guy but work calls. Thanks so much for hanging out with them today. It sure makes things easier for us."

"You're welcome, I'm happy to do it."

A little later in the morning Christie woke up and joined Westin and Michelle in the living room. She was smiling, "Good morning!"

Michelle was holding Westin, "Good morning! He is such a good baby and a little sweetie."

Christie smiled and approached her little son. "He is such a good boy! Thanks, Michelle, for staying with us today. I'm really not supposed to be picking up much and especially Westin right now, but sometimes I get tempted."

Michelle smiled. "Well, that's what I'm here for today so plan on taking it easy."

Christie said, "Yes, ma'am."

That afternoon Christie received a phone call from her college friend, Michelle Castello. Michelle lives in Bartlett, Illinois, a suburb of Chicago. Michelle is a nurse practitioner and had been in contact with Andrea quite a bit when Christie was first in the hospital, as well as reaching out to Christie throughout her hospital stays leading up to her surgery. Christie answered her phone, "Hi! So, are you going to be able to come here?"

She was excited and hopeful that her friend was calling to say that she would be able to.

Michelle smiled on the other end. "Yes! I will be there tomorrow. You will need to text me your parents' address so I can put it in my GPS."

Christie said, "No problem, I'll do that right away. It's going to be so good to see you!"

Michelle told her friend, "I can't wait. I'll see you tomorrow. Love you!"

"I love you too!" Christie hung up the phone and sat there for a moment and thought, *It's going to be so good to see her.*

Christie had good talks with Michelle throughout the day as well as with her uncle Joe who stopped by to see how things were going. Westin was a good baby all day long and Michelle really enjoyed her time with them. She even mentioned to Christie and the others, "Christie, you look so good. You look so good on the outside that no one would ever guess what you have been going through on the inside. You're amazing!" Everyone echoed Michelle's sentiments.

John received a phone call from his aunt Lora that his uncle Gary was at the farm along with his son, Jarid, and Jarid's children, Maesyn and Rafe. John asked if they were going to stop by, but Gary didn't want to be too much trouble. John insisted that they come over as soon as he knew Jarid and the kids were along. They stopped in and all enjoyed the mini-reunion.

That evening John's aunt Linda Bredberg along with her sister Lora Bain dropped by, so that Linda could get instructions on her duties for tomorrow, and of course her real reason was to see firsthand how her great-niece was doing and to meet her great great-nephew. Lora, since she had to work each day, was there to ensure she got her "Westin Time."

"Christie, you look so good!" Linda gave Christie a hug.

Christie smiled. "Thank you. I feel pretty good."

Linda went on, "You have been through so much. You are so fortunate. I'm so happy that you are going to be okay. How does it feel to have that defibrillator inside you?"

Christie thanked her great-aunt and said, "It's taken some getting used to. At first it felt humongous! It's moved a little bit too since it has been installed but all in all I'm getting used to it. It's a good insurance policy if something were to happen again with my heart."

Linda replied, "Oh yes."

As Christie lied down in bed for the evening, she called Brian to wish him a good night's sleep. "Hello, Love. Are you thinking about going to sleep?"

Brian responded to his wife, "Hi, Love. Yeah, I'm pretty tired and am getting ready to call it a day."

"Well, before you go to sleep, I've got good news!"

"What's that?"

"Michelle is driving down here tomorrow to come see us!"

Brian smiled. "Good deal! Tell Ratchet I said hey."

Christie scolded Brian, "Quit calling her 'Ratchet'! I will tell her you said hello but I won't be calling her Ratchet."

Brian chuckled, "Okay, but she will be disappointed."

"Yeah right. I love you."

"I love you too."

43

August 21, 2019

John's aunt Linda arrived around 6:45 a.m. John thanked her for being able to spend the day with Christie and Westin. "Oh, I'm happy to do so. We are going to have a nice day."

John said, "If you are having any trouble with Westin, don't hesitate to call for Christie. She needs her rest but she also wants to be here for him."

Linda said, "Okay, I will keep that in mind. He is a good little baby. I'm sure we will be fine."

John smiled. "I'm sure you will be too."

Linda asked, "What time did Andrea leave for work this morning?"

John said, "That lady left at four thirty this morning."

Linda said, "She has to be worn out with everything that's going on."

John nodded. "She is, but considering what Christie has been through, she wouldn't have it any other way. I try to make sure she has been getting as much sleep as possible by taking care of Westin overnight. Plus, I really enjoy that."

Linda smiled and said, "I bet you do." John headed on to work knowing his aunt had everything under control.

Christie awoke around 8:30 a.m. and joined her great-aunt Linda and Westin in the living room. Linda was making faces and goofy noises at Westin, and he was laughing at this new person entertaining him.

Christie said, "Well, well, it sounds like someone is having a good time!"

Linda smiled. "Good morning, Christie, we sure are!"

Christie smiled. "Have you been a good boy for Aunt Linda?"

Westin smiled at his mom and Linda said, "He sure has."

Christie said, "I'm glad to hear that."

The two women talked and got caught up. They hadn't spoken in person since last December when Christie, Brian, and Natalie came up for Christmas; and Andrea held a baby shower for Christie at the same time. In fact that was the last time Christie saw Michelle Castello in person. Christie told Linda how excited she was that her friend was coming today. Linda was happy for Christie.

Michelle arrived around 10:30 a.m. She was anxious to see Christie in person to evaluate how she is doing. She has been very concerned for her friend. Christie opened the door of the house as Michelle was exiting her car. "Hey, hey!"

Michelle looked toward the door. "Hey! It's so good to see you!" She quickly walked toward Christie and the two friends gave each other a hug.

"Come on in," Christie said to Michelle.

Once inside Christie introduced Michelle to Linda. Linda said, "Oh, I remember meeting you at Christie's baby shower. It's nice to see you again."

Michelle responded, "It's nice to see you too."

Christie picked up Westin, even though she wasn't supposed to do that, and turned him toward Michelle. "This is Westin. Westin, this is Aunt Chell."

Michelle smiled and took the baby from Christie, "Well hello, Westin, it's so nice to meet you."

Westin stared at Michelle and smiled at yet another new person he was getting to meet.

John was parked in his car underneath a shade tree at a local park in Washington. He had just finished his lunch and was listening to the radio. He received a text from Christie, "I'm not sure if you already had lunch but we are headed to Unc & Neph's for lunch."

John smiled, even though he had just had his lunch, Unc & Neph's was close by where he was and he headed up there to visit with Christie and her entourage.

John joined Christie, Michelle, Linda, and Westin at their table. He gave Michelle a hug and told her it was nice to see her again and wished he could spend more time with her. Michelle smiled and said she would make sure she had more time on her next visit.

John visited with the ladies and his little grandson for a while and then announced, "Well, I have to get moving. I am scheduled to record a client in a little while and I need to be on time."

All said goodbye. On his way out, John stopped by the bar and paid for the ladies' lunch bill. He smiled as he walked out the door.

When the ladies and the little baby got back home, they visited a little while longer and then it was time for Michelle to head back home. She had around a four-hour drive ahead of her.

Christie said to her friend, "I'm so happy that you got to come today. You drove such a long time and then have to do it again now, I'm sorry."

Michelle smiled at her friend. "You don't have to be sorry. I wanted to come see you and Westin. I'm so thankful to see how well you are doing! You have been through a lot."

Christie hugged her friend. Michelle said goodbye to Westin and Linda and headed back home to Bartlett.

Christie asked Linda if she was okay with her lying down and taking a rest.

Linda said, "Of course, definitely. Go lay down and take a nap. We will be fine."

Christie thanked her great-aunt and went to her bedroom to get some rest.

A couple of hours later, the Bain home received a visit from another well-wisher. It was Linda's sister Barb Smith, from Davenport. She had been worried and concerned over Christie, and when she found out Christie was in Iowa, she had to come see her and to meet Westin, of course.

Christie woke up and came into the living room. She was happy to see her great-aunt Barb, "Aunt Barb! Hello!"

Barb smiled at Christie and they gave each other a hug. Barb said, "It's so good to see you! I have been told you are doing much better."

Christie smiled. "Yes, I am getting stronger."

Barb said, "I'm so happy that you are." She turned to look at Westin who was being held by Linda, "Now this little guy is so precious. I love his curls."

Christie said, "Thank you. He really is a good little baby."

A little while later Andrea arrived home. She was happy to see everyone having a good time and getting a good visit in. Lora stopped in for a little bit to get her "Westin Time" in and then she and her two sisters decided it was time to go. John, Andrea, and Christie thanked Linda for spending her day here. Linda said she really enjoyed it. Christie hugged her aunt. It had been a fun day.

That night Christie and Westin were already sleeping. John and Andrea were catching up on how things had been going at both of their jobs. Andrea said, "Now tomorrow I am working from home."

John said, "I know. The time is going too fast. You're going to be leaving me on Friday."

Andrea hugged her husband. "At least Christie is getting better. That's the most important thing right now."

John looked at his wife. "You are right. Thank God she is."

44

August 23, 2019

It was Friday. Time for Andrea, Christie, and Westin to head toward Hot Springs, Arkansas. It was also John and Andrea's thirty-third wedding anniversary.

Yesterday had been a nice day. Andrea was able to catch up on laundry in preparation for their departure today, as well as working from home for her job. John's mother, Beverly, drove down from Davenport, so that she could visit her granddaughter and hold her great-grandson. Christie was happy to see her grandma, and her grandma was so grateful to see that Christie was on the road to recovery.

"Happy anniversary, Sweet Cheeks!"

Andrea smiled at her husband. "Happy anniversary!"

John continued, "Now be careful on the roads, be safe."

Andrea said, "We will. We will let you know our progress throughout the day."

John looked at the love of his life and said, "When do you think you can come back home?"

Andrea told her husband, "I am thinking sometime next month. I want to help Christie with a few things, and I want to make sure she is cleared to lift Westin before I go. Otherwise, we will have to find her some help."

John nodded. "We may have to do that anyway."

Christie and Westin were ready. John and Andrea finished loading up her car and then got Westin secured. John hugged his daughter. "I love you, girl. I'm so proud of you. Keep doing what the doctors tell you." He was tearing up.

Christie looked at her dad, she was going to miss him too. "Dad, now don't start, everything is going to be okay."

John nodded his head at his daughter. "I know." John said goodbye to Westin and kissed his little cheeks and forehead. Westin smiled at his papa. John then hugged and kissed Andrea. The three headed on their way. John watched until he couldn't see the car and then got in his car and headed to work.

At 12:03 p.m., John received a text from Christie, "We just left Poplar Bluff, says we should be at the hotel around 3:45." John sent a "thumbs up" emoticon back to his daughter.

At 5:21 p.m. Christie sent her dad a text, "We got settled in a little bit ago and now Mom and Westin ran to grab baby wipes."

John texted back, "Very cool! How are you doing?"

Christie decided it would be easier to talk to her dad in case he had more questions.

John's phone rang. It was Christie. "Hello!"

Christie responded to her dad, "Hello. I'm doing good, just tired. It was a long trip."

John smiled on his end, "Yes, it is. I'm glad you get to stretch out and relax now. Are you really doing good?"

Christie got slightly irritated. "Dad, yes. I'm doing all right."

John didn't want to upset Christie but he thought to himself, all right isn't good.

John continued, "I'm sorry, I just worry about you. I'm so grateful for your progress."

Christie lightened up. "I know you are. I am watching out and doing what I'm supposed to do and when I get tired, I take a nap or at least try to relax."

John said, "That's the best thing to do."

Christie then told her dad, "I guess I better hang up so I can get a little sleep before Mom and Westin get back."

"That's a good idea, daughter. I love you."

Christie smiled and said, "I love you too. I'll talk to you later."

A few minutes later, Christie received a call from Brian. "Hi, Babe, we just pulled into the parking lot."

Christie was happy that she would soon be reunited with Brian and Natalie. She gave Brian the room number and Natalie and he were quickly at the door. Christie opened the door and Natalie yelled "Momma!" then she gave Christie a big hug.

"Hello, Sweetie, I'm so glad you are here!"

Natalie smiled and asked, "How is your heart doing, Momma?"

Christie smiled. "My heart is doing really good, Baby. I feel much better each day."

Natalie smiled. "I'm glad you are feeling better."

Brian shut the door and placed the bags on the floor. He looked at his wife and said, "Me too."

They gave each other a hug and kiss and then settled in.

45

August 24, 2019

It was a nice day in Hot Springs, Arkansas. Brian was excited to be attending the logging expo. He was also grateful to have his family with him.

There were all kinds of different vendors from the logging industry displaying their products. The convention center is a big place but it didn't take much equipment on display to make it feel smaller.

Brian collected lots of literature from the different booths as they made their way throughout the event. He pushed Christie in the wheelchair that Andrea had arranged for her, and Natalie helped Gigi push Westin in his stroller. Christie was so thankful to be able to attend this event with Brian, since it was so important to him. They ran into several different people who Brian works with in the industry; including folks from Lone Star Truck Group. All were very kind and happy to see Christie out of the hospital and attending the expo.

At one end of the convention center, the happy family came upon a chainsaw wood carver who was demonstrating how to sculpt wood with a chainsaw. Several people gathered around in amazement at the carver's talent.

Natalie noticed a cute carving of a bear about a foot tall. She fell in love with it. "Daddy, can I have this?"

Brian looked at his little girl and then looked at the bear, "I guess you can. What should we get for your mom?"

Natalie looked around at the carvings of bears, birds, and other animals and then she noticed a pine tree about two feet tall. "How about this, Daddy?"

Brian smiled. "Sure." He paid for the carvings and Natalie walked a little taller holding her bear with pride.

Christie was very thankful to have the wheelchair. She knew that she would not have had the stamina to walk around this place all day long. "Thanks for getting this for me, Mom."

Andrea smiled. Her feet were starting to hurt her. It had been a lot of walking. "Oh, you're welcome, Honey."

The group happened along and met up with their friends Brad and Barbara Keener and their college student daughter, Jacie. The Keeners were so happy to see Christie and told her how worried they had been and how good it was to see her here looking so well. Christie hugged them and thanked them. Natalie showed off her little brother to them and Gigi was happy to see them all again. Brad is a timber buyer and does a lot of business with Brian and his dad.

Brad said, "Are you guys getting hungry? We were just getting ready to go to that Mexican restaurant down the street."

The Firths and Andrea looked at each other and Brian said, "Sure, that sounds like a good idea."

The two families had a nice visit, and Christie asked the Keeners to join them tonight for a magic show. There were a limited number of tickets left, and she was getting ready to purchase them on her phone. Jacie thought that sounded like a great idea, and Brad and Barbara accepted Christie's offer.

Natalie smiled and said, "I can't wait to go to the magic show!"

The group laughed and decided on when and where to meet before the big show.

It was a wonderful day at the logging expo. The family headed back to the hotel to rest up for their big night.

At dinner time they met the Keeners at DeLuca's Pizzeria. Brad insisted on paying for lunch this afternoon and now he wasn't letting Brian cover the dinner bill. He tried to pay for the magic show but the Firths would have none of that. The entertainment was on them.

They had a very good meal and then headed down the street to Max Blades Theater of Magic.

The show was spectacular! There were all kinds of bright lights and loud music throughout. While Natalie and the others were mesmerized by all of the tricks and magic, little Westin fell asleep. He already had a busy day at the expo and seeing all of the sights and sounds there. He would have to take a pass on this magic show.

46

The week of August 26, Christie continued to heal. She still tired easily but her stamina was improving. Dr. Hayes added another medicine to her daily regimen. It was helping.

Christie and Andrea had been frustrated that they hadn't made any progress regarding her medical plane bill. With a $120,500.00 bill looming it was sometimes hard for Christie to rest easy.

Then, finally on Tuesday, September 3, things started to happen. Christie and Andrea were both on their phones at the same time. Christie speaking to a representative of Blue Cross Blue Shield and Andrea speaking to a representative of Pafford EMS.

Christie explained, "I didn't have much choice in the matter. I had to get to the Cleveland Clinic quickly. My doctor arranged for this plane. If it wasn't necessary, he wouldn't have done it."

The woman on the other end replied, "Well, I just don't see where this is a financial responsibility of Blue Cross Blue Shield."

Shortly after the woman replied, Andrea waved at Christie, muted her phone and told her, "Hang up! Just hang up. Don't say anything. I've got a person on my line that is taking care of it."

Christie couldn't believe what her mother was saying to her, but she acted like a good daughter and listened to her mom and hung up the phone.

Christie sat down next to her mom and listened. Andrea continued, "Oh yes, thank you so much! Yes, she is healing well. We are truly blessed. Thanks again. Bye, bye." Andrea looked at Christie and yelled, "Yay! It's all covered. Your insurance is taking care of the bill for the plane!"

Christie looked at her mom with a sigh of relief. "How did that happen? This whole time they said they weren't covering it. What changed?"

Andrea smiled. "The plane company said that they have settled with Blue Cross Blue Shield and they are writing off $48,000.00 of the cost and that Blue Cross Blue Shield is picking up the rest.

Christie hugged her mom. "Thank goodness, you got through to her!"

Andrea smiled. "Yes!"

Christie laughed. "I wonder what that other woman thought when I hung up on her?"

47

Andrea has been noticing measurable signs of improvement with Christie. She knew at some point she needed to leave so that Christie can get back to being confident in taking care of herself and Westin on her own. Christie has been doing more and more for Westin, and Andrea has been there when she needed her but for the most part, she was doing it all herself.

Andrea asked Christie, "What would you think if I headed for home this weekend?"

Christie gave her mom a quizzical look, "You mean for good?"

Andrea gave a small smile at her daughter and said, "Yes."

Christie looked at her mom and said, "Well, we have to try it sometime."

Andrea reassured her daughter, "Let's give it a try and if you need us to come back down, we will be here for you."

Christie nodded and said, "Okay."

That evening Andrea called John. "Are you ready for a roommate again?"

John asked his wife, "What do you mean?"

Andrea continued, "I'm planning on coming home this Saturday."

John asked, "You mean for good?"

Andrea said, "Yes, I think it's time for me to come back. Christie is doing very well, and I think it's best for me to go so that she can gain her confidence even more. I told her if she needs us, we can come back down."

John smiled and told his wife, "We are all so blessed, I think that's wonderful! Are you okay?"

Andrea told John, "Yes, I'm okay."

Saturday morning, September 7, arrived very quickly. Andrea had packed her things the night before and had most everything loaded in her car. It was 4:30 a.m. She stood over Westin's crib and watched the little boy sleeping. He has grown so much while she was here. She wondered to herself, *How can I leave him? How can I leave them?* She knew she had to do so. This was their place and her place was back home in Iowa. She blew her sleeping grandson a kiss and went into the living room.

Christie and Brian were sitting in the living room when Andrea walked out. Christie smiled at her mom. "Today is the big day."

Andrea smiled back. "Yes, it is. Are you going to be able to take care of this little boy over here?" She pointed at Brian.

Brian laughed. "Hey!"

Christie stood up and told her mom, "Mom, I'm okay, and I'm going to stay okay."

Andrea nodded at her daughter and gave her a hug. "I know you are. You are awesome! Just remember, if you need me here, I will be here. I expect to talk to you every day."

Christie teared up. "I know and you will. Thank you for everything, Mom. I don't know what we would have done if you weren't here. I love you."

"I love you too, Peanut." Andrea headed to the door and Brian followed her out carrying her bag.

When they reached Andrea's car, Brian placed the bag inside and told his mother-in-law, "I don't know what to say or where to start. You have been here through all of this. You have taken care of Christie as well as the kids and me. Can't you stay a little longer?"

Andrea gave Brian a hug and said, "You take care of my daughter and those grandkids."

Brian said that he would and then he said, "Thank you."

Andrea said, "You're welcome and you don't have to thank me. Thank you for letting me help." She got in her car and headed down their long driveway back to Iowa.

Time passed and some days Christie felt great and others not so much so. She had several visits to Dr. Hayes's office. Sometimes she met with Charles Shoalmire, nurse practitioner. She had more echocardiograms and her ejection fraction was low, in the thirties. Different medications were tried but didn't seem to be improving things. Christie kept positive thoughts through this difficult time and she continued to treat it as an obstacle course that she would someday conquer.

On October 22, she met again with nurse practitioner Charles Shoalmire. Charles walked into the examination room. "Hello, Christie, how are you feeling today?"

Christie smiled. "I feel great! I am looking forward to seeing what the echocardiogram finds today because I really do feel a lot better."

Charles looked at Christie and said, "I'm sorry but I don't think an echo is necessary today. I believe we need to get you on the list for a heart transplant and have you start going to the heart failure clinic."

Christie was having none of this. "But I really do feel different. In a good way. Could you please do the test?"

Charles gave in and went forward with the echocardiogram.

During the process he was quite surprised at how things looked and what her EF rate was. She was in the forties. A few minutes after the procedure, Charles came back in the room and said to Christie; "Your ejection fraction rate is too good to be on a heart transplant list."

Christie smiled. "Thank you for doing the echo. I knew I was feeling better."

Charles smiled. "You're welcome. I don't have an explanation on why they have changed so much for the better."

The next morning, Christie was at home. Her phone rang. It was Dr. Hayes's office. "Hello."

"Hi, Christie?"

"Yes."

"This is Cheryl from Dr. Hayes's office. Dr. Hayes is very happy, your tests look great!"

Christie smiled. "Thank you. He thought they were good?"

Cheryl replied, "Yes, you are to keep doing what you are doing."

Christie thanked Cheryl. The next thing she did was sent a text to her mom and dad, "I got a call from Cheryl the nurse at Dr. Hayes office she said the test looked great and Dr. Hayes was very happy!"

John quickly replied to his daughter, "You've made my day! That is awesome news!!"

That evening John and Andrea called Christie and Brian. Christie told them that the doctors didn't have an explanation for her turn around. The parents listened intently. John said, "I know why. You are a miracle!"

48

November 27, 2019

The day before Thanksgiving Day. John and Andrea were excited! Tomorrow they would be celebrating Thanksgiving with their family here at their home in Iowa. Sean would be here and so would Christie with Brian and the kids. Westin's first Thanksgiving!

It was 8:00 a.m., Andrea received a text from Christie, "We should be there in fifteen minutes or so."

Andrea texted back, "Great! Drive careful." Christie promised they would.

The Firth family arrived shortly after. Once parked, John opened the door for Natalie and she leapt into his arms. "Hi. Papa!"

John smiled and hugged his granddaughter, "Hi, Natalie, welcome back!"

She said, "Thanks!"

Andrea was hugging Christie and Brian and looking in the back of their vehicle for Westin. "Where is my little man?"

Westin smiled at his Gigi. It was a precious reunion.

Brian and Christie were tired from their drive and went to bed shortly after arriving. John and Andrea served breakfast to Natalie and doted on Westin. They had a lot to be thankful for and they both knew it.

Thanksgiving arrived and Andrea made a delicious tender turkey with all of the fixings. The extended family of guests brought desserts and other side dishes. It was a modern-day cornucopia of a feast.

They had a houseful; besides John, Andrea, Sean, Christie, Brian, Natalie, and Westin; the feast included Joe Bain, his girlfriend Michelle Kline, Chris Carlson and his daughter Hope, Joni and Bruce DeMoss and their children Addy and Joe, Michelle's mother, Shirley Kline, and John, Joni and Joe's mother, Beverly, along with her friend Bernie.

The family had a great day. The house was abuzz with all sorts of activities from playing dice games to the kids running back and forth from the basement to the first floor. Football was enjoyed and the whole house was filled with joyful noise.

Before dinner, all gathered around the dining room table, there were also card tables set up in the living room, and John did his best to make a speech. "I just want to say that today is the day that we give thanks for all of our blessings." Everyone was looking at John and he made the mistake of looking at them, and particular at Christie. He could feel the love in the room and he started to choke up. He continued, "I'm going to get through this and say this, I am so thankful for all of you and for the fact that our Christie is here with us today." He paused and tightened his mouth shut and tried not to cry, but a tear rolled down his cheek. It's been a crazy year for us and I thank the good Lord for his grace and again for all of you."

Someone yelled out, "Here, here!" and others said, "Amen."

After all the guests had departed and Andrea, Sean, Christie, Brian, and Natalie had gone to bed; John sat in his recliner holding the sleeping little Westin. John was so happy and acknowledged how blessed that he and all of them are. He looked at little Westin and thought to himself, *That's my grandson!* He wondered what Westin would do for an occupation when he grew up. All kinds of ideas went through his head. Then he said to himself, "Whatever you end up doing for a living, it will be second to the fact that you will be a good man."

John then thought of 1 Corinthians 13, I may be able to speak the languages of men and even of angels, but if I have no love, my speech is no more than a noisy gong or a clanging bell. I may have the gift of inspired preaching; I may have all knowledge and understand all secrets; I may have all the faith needed to move mountains-but if

I have no love, I am nothing. I may give away everything I have, and even give up my body to be burned—but if I have no love, this does me no good. Love is patient and kind; it is not jealous or conceited or proud; love is not ill-mannered or selfish or irritable; love does not keep a record of wrongs; love is not happy with evil, but is happy with the truth. Love never gives up; and its faith, hope, and patience never fail.

Love is eternal. There are inspired messages, but they are temporary; there are gifts of speaking in strange tongues, but they will cease; there is knowledge, but it will pass.

For our gifts of knowledge and of inspired messages are only partial; but when what is perfect comes, then what is partial will disappear.

When I was a child, my speech, feelings, and thinking were all those of a child; now that I am a man, I have no more use for childish ways.

What we see now is like a dim image in a mirror; then we shall see face-to-face. What I know now is only partial; then it will be complete—as complete as God's knowledge of me.

Meanwhile these three remain: faith, hope, and love; and the greatest of these is love.

By the grace of God, the beat goes on,
Christie's journey continues…

ABOUT THE AUTHOR

John R. Bain is a thirty-three-year television and radio broad-cast veteran who is now retired. He resides with his wife, Andrea, on the Bain family farm in Wayland, Iowa.